# LAMENTATIONS

## VOLUME 7A

THE ANCHOR BIBLE is a fresh approach to the world's greatest classic. Its object is to make the Bible accessible to the modern reader; its method is to arrive at the meaning of biblical literature through exact translation and extended exposition, and to reconstruct the ancient setting of the biblical story, as well as the circumstances of its transcription and the characteristics of its transcribers.

THE ANCHOR BIBLE is a project of international and interfaith scope. Protestant, Catholic, and Jewish scholars from many countries contribute individual volumes. The project is not sponsored by any ecclesiastical organization and is not intended to reflect any particular theological doctrine. Prepared under our joint supervision, THE ANCHOR BIBLE is an effort to make available all the significant historical and linguistic knowledge which bears on the interpretation of the biblical record.

THE ANCHOR BIBLE is aimed at the general reader with no special formal training in biblical studies; yet, it is written with the most exacting standards of scholarship, reflecting the highest technical accomplishment.

This project marks the beginning of a new era of cooperation among scholars in biblical research, thus forming a common body of knowledge to be shared by all.

*William Foxwell Albright*
*David Noel Freedman*
GENERAL EDITORS

# THE ANCHOR BIBLE

# LAMENTATIONS

◆

## A New Translation with Introduction and Commentary

SECOND, REVISED EDITION

## DELBERT R. HILLERS

THE ANCHOR BIBLE

Doubleday

New York  London  Toronto  Sydney  Auckland

The Anchor Bible
PUBLISHED BY DOUBLEDAY
a division of Bantam Doubleday Dell Publishing Group, Inc.
666 Fifth Avenue, New York, New York 10103

THE ANCHOR BIBLE, DOUBLEDAY, and the portrayal
of an anchor with the letters AB are trademarks of
Doubleday, a division of Bantam Doubleday Dell Publishing
Group, Inc.

LIBRARY OF CONGRESS CATALOGING-IN-PUBLICATION DATA

Bible. O.T. Lamentations. English. Hillers. 1992.
　　Lamentations : a new translation with introduction and commentary
/ Delbert R. Hillers.
　　　　p.　　cm.—(The Anchor Bible ; v. 7A)
　　Includes bibliographical references and indexes.
　　1. Bible. O.T. Lamentations—Commentaries. I. Hillers, Delbert R.　　II. Title.
III. Series: Bible. English. Anchor Bible. 1964 ; v. 7A.
BS1533　1992
220.7'7 s—dc20　　　　　　　　　　　　　　　　　　　　91-17533
[224'.3077]　　　　　　　　　　　　　　　　　　　　　　　CIP


ISBN 0-385-26407-0

October 1992

10　9　8　7　6　5　4　3　2　1

*To the memory*
*of*
*my parents*

# CONTENTS

◆

# CONTENTS

# PREFACE

♦

I have written the following commentary primarily for the general reader, and have included only a limited amount of technical detail. As a result I do not always give explicit credit to the scholar who first proposed a given idea, and, although I cite some differing points of view on controverted issues, I do not always quote the full range of varying opinions. Let it be stated here, then, that I am conscious of my great debt to the many scholars, living and dead, who have occupied themselves with Lamentations, and that I hope my own commentary will attract at least some readers to look further into the extensive and excellent literature on this small book.

To the late William F. Albright, who in his lifetime performed so many acts of kindness and generosity toward me, I am also indebted for the opportunity to work on this interesting segment of the Anchor Bible project. General Editor David Noel Freedman read a draft of the commentary and eliminated many of my blunders and made numerous helpful suggestions. Here and there in the following pages I have expressly acknowledged his contributions, but this does not adequately express the degree to which I am indebted to him. I am grateful also to Phyllis Rimbach, who typed the final manuscript. A part of the reading for this commentary was done in the library of the École Biblique in Jerusalem, which hospitably opened its doors to this American visitor as it has to so many others.

# PREFACE TO THE
# SECOND EDITION

◆

I am indebted again to the general editor of the Anchor Bible, David Noel Freedman, this time for the opportunity to prepare a revised commentary on Lamentations, and for his critical reading of the manuscript, which eliminated many of my errors, supplied many things I had omitted, and contained numerous stimulating and useful suggestions. While trying to retain the general character and dimensions of the previous work, I have added new material to the bibliography and made revisions at those points where, on returning to study of the book, I find my views have most changed. I am grateful to reviewers of the first edition, whose generous and searching discussions have served as a stimulus and correction. Special thanks are due to Bruce Metzger, of the Princeton Theological Seminary, for supplying me with advance galleys of the *New Revised Standard Version* of Lamentations, and to Alan Cooper of Hebrew Union College, Cincinnati, for permitting me to read his manuscript on the message of Lamentations. I am indebted to Doris Gottschalk for typing the text and to Edwin Hostetter, who assisted with checking references.

The commentary of Claus Westermann *(Die Klagelieder: Forschungsgeschichte und Auslegung.* Neukirchen-Vluyn: Neukirchener, 1990), which reached my hands too late for incorporation in the commentary, is commended to interested readers, both for the distinguished author's own views and for its valuable and judicious survey of the history of interpretation of Lamentations.

# PRINCIPAL ABBREVIATIONS

◆

| | |
|---|---|
| Akk | Akkadian |
| ANET | J. B. Pritchard, ed., *Ancient Near Eastern Texts Relating to the Old Testament*, 3d ed. (Princeton, 1969) |
| Ar | Arabic |
| Aram | Aramaic |
| BA | *Biblical Archaeologist* |
| BDB | F. Brown, S. R. Driver, and C. A. Briggs, eds., of Wilhelm Gesenius's *Hebrew and English Lexicon of the Old Testament*, 2d ed. (Oxford, 1952) |
| BETL | Bibliotheca ephemeridum theologicarum lovaniensium |
| BHK³ | R. Kittel, ed., *Biblia hebraica*, 3d ed. (Stuttgart, 1937) |
| BHS | *Biblia hebraica Stuttgartensia* |
| BZAW | Beihefte zur *Zeitschrift für die alttestamentliche Wissenschaft* |
| CAD | *The Assyrian Dictionary of the Oriental Institute of the University of Chicago* (the *Chicago Assyrian Dictionary*) (Chicago, 1956–) |
| CBQ | *Catholic Biblical Quarterly* |
| CTA | Andrée Herdner, *Corpus des tablettes en cunéiformes alphabétiques* (Paris, 1963) |
| E | English version, when chapter and/or verse numbers differ from the Hebrew |
| Eth | Ethiopic |
| GKC | *Gesenius' Hebrew Grammar*, ed. E. Kautzsch, rev. and trans. A. E. Cowley, 2d English ed. (Oxford, 1910) |
| Gr | Greek |
| Heb | Hebrew |
| HTR | *Harvard Theological Review* |

# PRINCIPAL ABBREVIATIONS

| | |
|---|---|
| IEJ | *Israel Exploration Journal* |
| JAAR | *Journal of the American Academy of Religion* |
| JBL | *Journal of Biblical Literature* |
| JCS | *Journal of Cuneiform Studies* |
| JJS | *Journal of Jewish Studies* |
| JNES | *Journal of Near Eastern Studies* |
| JQR | *Jewish Quarterly Review* |
| JTS | *Journal of Theological Studies* |
| KB³ | Ludwig Koehler and Walter Baumgartner, *Lexikon in Veteris Testamenti Libros*, 3d ed. (Leiden, 1967) |
| NJV | *New Jewish Version* |
| NRSV | *New Revised Standard Version* |
| Phoen | Phoenician |
| RHR | *Revue de l'histoire des religions* |
| RSV | *Revised Standard Version* |
| Syr | Syriac |
| ThR | *Theologische Rundschau* |
| TLZ | *Theologische Literaturzeitung* |
| Ug | Ugaritic |
| UT | Cyrus H. Gordon, *Ugaritic Textbook* (Rome, 1965) |
| VT | *Vetus Testamentum* |
| ZAW | *Zeitschrift für die alttestamentliche Wissenschaft* |
| ZS | *Zeitschrift für Semitistik und verwandte Gebiete* |

# Introduction

♦

# To Remember and to Hope

> In the fifth month, the seventh day of the month, in the nineteenth year of King Nebuchadnezzar, king of Babylon, Nebuzaradan, captain of the guard, an official of the king of Babylon, entered Jerusalem. He burned down the house of the Lord and the king's house; and all the houses in Jerusalem, all around. . . . The rest of the people who were left in the city, and those who had deserted to the king of Babylon, and the rest of the populace, Nebuzaradan, captain of the guard, took to Babylon as prisoners. The captain of the guard left only some of the poorest in the country to tend the vines and farm the land. (2 Kgs 25:8–12)*

This passage from the second book of Kings is one kind of account of what happened when Jerusalem fell to the Babylonians, in 587 B.C.E. It is prose, and is full of concrete detail, down to dates and names.

The book of Lamentations also has as its theme the fall of Jerusalem, but it is obviously a different sort of composition. Dates and names are lacking, and there is no sequential ordering of the events, as in Kings. Far from being prose, Lamentations is verse. In fact, it is one of the most elaborate compositions in the Bible, its five chapters being full of poetic artifice and convention.

---

* The translation of this Bible passage, and of others throughout the commentary, is my own, except in cases where an individual English version is cited for a specific purpose and identified (e.g. NRSV).

3

# INTRODUCTION

Why poetry amid the ruins of the city? What purpose was Lamentations meant to serve?

Lamentations is a recital of the horrors and atrocities of the long siege and its aftermath, and, beyond the tale of physical sufferings, an account of the spiritual significance of the fall of the city. For the ancient people chosen by the Lord the fall of Jerusalem meant the destruction of every cherished symbol of their election by God. In line after line the poet recalls all of the precious, sacred things that had been lost or shattered: the city itself, once "the perfection of beauty, the joy of the whole earth"; the city walls and towers, once the outward sign that "God is in the midst of her"; the king, "the anointed of the LORD,[1] the breath of our nostrils"; the priests, and with them all festive and solemn worship; the prophets, and with them all visions and the living word of God; the land itself, Israel's property granted her by God, now turned over to strangers; the people—dead, exiled, or slaves in their own land. Every sign that had once provided assurance and confidence in God was gone.

Thus Lamentations was meant to serve the survivors of the catastrophe simply as an *expression* of the horror and grief they felt. People live on best after calamity, not by utterly repressing their grief and shock, but by facing it, and by measuring its dimensions.

One such dimension was guilt. Lamentations is also a confession, and testimony to a search for absolution. Those who survived knew or felt themselves, as individuals or as part of an imperfect human community, somehow responsible for the ruin of their city, their land, and their temple.

The fact that Lamentations is verse begins to find its explanation here. Poetic form serves to set off the words of a text from ordinary words, to remind us by its very artificiality that we are not dealing with reality directly, but as reshaped and structured by human invention and skill. To face an utterly chaotic experience of

[1] As is well known, the name of the god of Israel, Yahweh, came to be avoided in the course of time, even in worship, and a different word, meaning "Lord," was substituted for it in reading the Scriptures. The effect of this substitution can already be seen in our earliest extant witnesses to the text of Lamentations (see the NOTE on 1:14). In the translation of Lamentations that follows, and in quotations of it (not otherwise), I have followed the venerable practice of using English "LORD" where the Tetragrammaton, YHWH, stands in the MT.

4

loss, ruin, and guilt, even in memory and retelling, may be devastating. The same experiences reworked into a sculpture, or a painting, or a poem, may enable survivors, and their descendants, to remember and contemplate their loss—not coolly, not without emotion—but without unbearable and measureless grief.

The poems of Lamentations also make the experience of the city's loss universal, in two senses. The mourning is for the common loss, and it seems fitting that here there are no names of the slain, no private griefs. The poetry of Lamentations universalizes the fall of the city in a second way also. By drawing on a tradition of poems about the fall of human cities and about how they are abandoned by their gods, it helps transform an event that otherwise, in the context of the centuries of ancient history, would seem neither unusual nor statistically important. Furthermore, the very form of the poetry does its part in enabling more remote generations, with their own griefs and guilts, to find here warning or comfort in a language that is, paradoxically, common and enduringly contemporary.[2]

In other words, the poems in Lamentations were written to serve in ritual. We have no way of knowing whether such use in ritual was, initially, only the solitary observance of the writers or whether the fresh poems were adopted at once by some community. In either case the language and form of the text are aimed at remembrance and repetition commensurate with the need not to forget and to live on.

Central to the book, and to the intent of the ritual, is the expression and strengthening of hope. It is the merit of Lamentations that it does not quickly or easily promise away the present agony. It does not encourage the remnant of Israel to take comfort in the fathers, or the Exodus, or the land, or Zion, or the line of David, or any of the old symbols of her status with God. The series

---

[2] Cohen (1982: 20) summarizes rabbinic interpretation of Lamentations as found in *Lamentations Rabbati*, and describes how this biblical book, in its setting on the 9th of Ab, was taken as "the eternal lament for all Jewish catastrophes, past, present, and future." Mintz (1982: 1) describes the writer of Lamentations as "*burdened* by long-used traditions of communal laments and funereal songs" (italics mine). Although this is not an incorrect or unfair observation, from a certain point of view, yet it seems to me that the author turns this "burden" into an advantage.

of "mighty acts of God" toward Israel had ended with an unmistakable act of judgment, so that the nation's history could be no source of hope. Nor does it at any point forecast a speedy turn in the fortunes of Israel. Instead the book offers, in its central chapter, the example of an unnamed man who has suffered under the hand of God. To sketch this typical sufferer, this "Everyman," it draws on the language and ideas of the psalms of individual lament, a tradition quite separate from the national history. From near despair, this man wins through to confidence that God's mercy is not at an end, and that his final, inmost will for man is not suffering. From this beginning of hope the individual turns to call the nation to penitent waiting for God's mercy.

# LITURGICAL USE OF LAMENTATIONS

Although direct evidence for liturgical use of Lamentations is not available until the Christian era, the poems contained in it may have been used in public mourning over the destruction of Jerusalem immediately after they were written, and thus soon after the events treated in the book. Both the poetic forms found in the book and the organization of the poems fit Lamentations for "ritual" in the broad sense, in which many a poem is an abstraction from experience that invites contemplation, repetition, and the participation of others besides the author. But also in the narrower sense the poems are eminently suited for ritual in that they contain elements common in religious rites, such as petition, lament, confession, and imprecation, and draw on ancient native traditions of compositions for common worship, such as the psalms of lament.

Nothing in the poems precludes such a use. Although some scholars have raised doubts on this point, common readers with some experience in public worship may well trust their own judgment on this point. Formal characteristics, such as the use of "I" in many passages, do not rule out the idea that they were written, or at least soon used, in corporate worship, nor does the use of acrostic form compel us to think that chapters 1–4 were intended only for private study and devotion.[3]

[3] So Segert; cf. Westermann (1989: 305): acrostic form makes such compositions "more to be read than heard."

# INTRODUCTION

We cannot, of course, attempt anything like a reconstruction of "The Order of Service for Lamentation over Jerusalem," an enterprise in dramaturgy that some have attempted on the basis of the alternation among various speakers in some of the poems. Nor can we plausibly suppose that there existed a fixed liturgical practice of "Lament over the Ruined Sanctuary" already in preexilic times, and that the canonical book of Lamentations results from the continuation of this sort of established practice. The (mostly lost) lament tradition on which the present book draws seems to have been of a rather different sort (see below, "Lamentations and the City-Lament Tradition").

Public mourning over the destroyed city was carried on from earliest times. Jer 41:5, narrating an event just after the death of Gedaliah, the governor who was installed over Judah by the Chaldeans, tells of "eighty men from Shechem, Shiloh, and Samaria who had shaved off their beards, torn their garments, and lacerated their skin," coming to make offering at the house of Yahweh in Jerusalem. Zech 7:3–5, dated to 518 B.C., hence shortly after the return from Exile, makes it clear that mourning and fasting in the fifth month (Ab) had been going on ever since the city fell. Zech 8:19 also refers to a fast in the fifth month. It is, therefore, reasonable to suppose that the Lamentations were used in connection with this regular public mourning already in the exilic period.

Presumably continuing this ancient practice, later Jewish usage assigns Lamentations a place in the public mourning on the 9th of Ab, the fifth month, which falls in July or August according to the modern calendar. The 9th is chosen in preference to strict adherence to either of the two biblical dates (2 Kgs 25:8–9 gives the 7th of Ab; Jer 52:12 gives the 10th) because of the tradition that the *second* temple fell to Titus on the 9th of Ab, and that again in A.D. 135 the fortress of Bar Kokhba, leader of the second Jewish revolt, fell to the Romans on that day.

In various Christian liturgies portions of Lamentations are used in services on Maundy Thursday, Good Friday, and Holy Saturday, a custom that has resulted in the composition of eloquent musical settings of the text.[4]

---

[4] An informative summary statement on liturgical use of Lamentations, along with a history of the interpretation of the book, is found in Provan 1990. Tigay

Contemporary compositions—such as Bernstein's "Jeremiah" Symphony (1942) for mezzo-soprano and orchestra, and Stravinsky's "Threni" (1958), for solo voices, chorus, and orchestra—testify to the continuing vitality and universal quality of the texts.

# The Name of the Book

In the Hebrew Bible Lamentations has the title 'ēkāh 'How', the initial word of the book. In the Babylonian Talmud, however (b. B. Bat. 14b), and in other early Jewish writings, the book is called qīnōt, that is, "Lamentations." The titles in the Greek Bible, threnoi, and in the Vulgate, threni, are translations of this Hebrew name. Quite frequently manuscripts and printed editions of the ancient translations will add to this descriptive title the words "of Jeremiah" or "of Jeremiah the prophet."

# Place in the Canon

The canonicity of Lamentations has never been a matter of dispute. The position of Lamentations in the canon of the Hebrew scriptures, however, is of some importance for the question of authorship. It is never placed among the Prophets, where the book of Jeremiah stands, but is always somewhere in the third division of the Hebrew canon, the Writings (Ketubim). Its exact position among the Writings has varied in different ages and in different communities. The Babylonian Talmud (b. B. Bat. 14b) records a very old tradition that lists the Writings "chronologically," that is, according to their traditional date; the five Scrolls (Megillot) are not grouped together, and Lamentations, which refers to the Babylonian captivity, comes near the end of the list, just before Daniel and Esther. Hebrew Bibles, however, reflect liturgical practice in that within the Writings they group the five short books (the "Scrolls," Megillot), which had come to be read in public worship

---

1971 has a more extended list of literary and musical compositions based on Lamentations.

on five important festivals. The edition commonly used in scholarly study today, *Biblia hebraica Stuttgartensia (BHS)*, is based on a manuscript of A.D. 1008 (Codex Leningradensis), which lists the Scrolls in "chronological" order: Ruth, Song of Songs (from when Solomon was young!), Ecclesiastes (from his old age), Lamentations, and Esther. In many manuscripts and printed Bibles, however, especially those used by Ashkenazic Jews, the order is that in which the festivals come in the calendar: Song of Songs (Passover); Ruth (Weeks, *Shabuot*, Pentecost), Lamentations (the 9th of Ab), Ecclesiastes (Tabernacles, Sukkot), and Esther (Purim).

The second major tradition puts Lamentations just after Jeremiah (Baruch comes between them in some cases). This is the order followed, for example, in the Septuagint (LXX), the ancient Greek translation of the Bible, in the Vulgate (Vg), Jerome's Latin translation, and in English Bibles commonly used among Christians. This order was anciently known to Josephus, as may be inferred from his account of the Hebrew canon (*Contra Apionem* 1.8), and is also followed by Melito of Sardis (d. 190; see Eusebius, *Historia ecclesiastica* 4.26.14) and by Origen (Eusebius 6.25.2). As Jerome explains, this listing fits an enumeration of the Old Testament books that makes their number agree with the letters of the Hebrew alphabet; "Jeremias cum Cinoth" counts as one book. Jerome, however, does mention the existence of a varying tradition, which put Lamentations and Ruth with the Writings ("Prologus Galeatus," *Patrologia latina* 28, cols. 593–604).

# THE DATE OF LAMENTATIONS

The view commonly held by modern scholars agrees closely with the traditional view, namely, that the book of Lamentations was written not long after the fall of Jerusalem in 587 B.C.E. The memory of the horrors of that event seems to be still fresh in the mind of the author or authors. Moreover, the book at no point testifies to a belief that things would soon change for the better; the kind of hope that appeared in later exilic times had not yet arisen.

Considerable scholarly effort has been expended on determining the order in which the five separate poems were written, but no consensus exists. One principal recent student of the book, Wilhelm Rudolph, has argued that chapter 1 must date from the first capture of Jerusalem by the Babylonians, that is, from shortly after 597, not from after 587 B.C.E. His main reason for this view, which has won some adherents, is that chapter 1 does not speak of the *destruction* of the city and temple as do the other chapters, but only of its capture.[5] This is essentially an argument from silence, and is not a secure basis for separating this poem from the others chronologically. Before Rudolph, other scholars argued for putting chapter 1 somewhat later than 2 and 4. Furthermore, the evidence of the new Babylonian Chronicle shows that the first siege must have been quite short,[6] which does not fit with the references in the chapter to severe famine (1:11, 19; see the commentary on v 11). Others have wanted to put chapter 3 later than the others because it has a less vivid description of events in the siege than that in 2 and 4. The truth is that there is insufficient evidence for a precise chronological ordering of the separate laments.[7]

The inconclusiveness of arguments about the sequence of composition of the five poems is consistent with the view taken in this commentary, that the style of the book is deliberately universalizing, using conventional and traditional descriptions of the fall of a city that, by their very nature and intent, resist efforts to treat them as documentary films of what happened.

# THE AUTHORSHIP OF LAMENTATIONS

That the prophet Jeremiah wrote Lamentations is so firmly rooted in traditions about the Bible, in western literature, and even in art that even after the ascription to Jeremiah was challenged

---

[5] See Rudolph's commentary on chapter 1 (1962) for details.

[6] See Malamat (1968:144–45) for a discussion of the chronology of the events, with reference to the Chronicle published by Wiseman in 1956.

[7] The idea that one or more chapters of Lamentations come from the Maccabean period was advanced by Fries (1893), but found few adherents. Lachs (1966–67) has revived the idea, but his arguments are equally unconvincing.

(first in 1712, by H. von der Hardt[8]), discussion of the book's authorship has tended to take the form of listing reasons why Jeremiah could not have written the book, or why he must have, as though the tradition were unanimous. Ancient tradition on this point is not in fact unanimous, however, and the problem of authorship may perhaps be best approached by first listing the separate traditions. Then, as though it were a problem of deciding between textual variants, we may ask: which tradition can best account for the origin of the other?

The first tradition does not name any author for the book and implies that it was not Jeremiah. This is the tradition represented by the Masoretic Text (MT), which says nothing whatever about the authorship of the book, and in which Lamentations is separated from Jeremiah and put among the Writings; for details see "Place in the Canon," above.

The second tradition is that Jeremiah wrote the book. The LXX prefixes these words to the first chapter: "And it came to pass that Jeremiah sat weeping and composed this lament over Jerusalem and said——." This heading in the Greek translation may possibly go back to a Hebrew original, for it is Semitic rather than Greek in style, though it is equally possible that a Greek editor imitated biblical diction here. In the LXX Lamentations is placed with other works associated with Jeremiah. The Vg follows the Greek closely, both in the ordering of the book and in the heading. The Targum (Aramaic translation) ascribes the book to Jeremiah, but more briefly and in different words. It is in accord with other Jewish tradition as recorded, for example, in the Babylonian Talmud (b. B. Bat. 15a). In rabbinic writings, passages from Lamentations are often introduced by "Jeremiah said." The heading in the Syriac version (Peshitta) titles the work: "The book of Lamentations of Jeremiah the prophet." The oldest of these ancient authorities is the LXX.

[8] Hardt proposed that the five chapters were written respectively by Daniel, Shadrach, Meshach, Abednego, and King Jehoiachin! (see Ricciotti 1924: 35). To say that modern critical opinion in this matter was anticipated by Ibn Ezra, as does Lachs (1966–67: 46–47), is erroneous. Ibn Ezra rejects only the rabbinic tradition that Lamentations was the scroll burned by Jehoiakim, but not Jeremiah's authorship of the book.

In spite of the great antiquity of this tradition, it is relatively easy to account for it as secondary to the other. In the first place, there was a very natural desire in the early days of biblical interpretation to determine the authorship of anonymous biblical books. As the one major prophetic figure active in Judah just before and after the fall of Jerusalem, Jeremiah was a candidate sufficiently qualified to meet the demands of a none-too-critical age, especially since certain of his words seemed to fit the theme of Lamentations: "O that my head were waters, and my eyes a fount of tears, that I might weep day and night for the slain of my people" (8:23 [=9:1E]). Second, there was an explicit statement in the Bible that Jeremiah wrote "laments" (2 Chr 35:25), which I translate here as literally as possible so that some of the difficulties of the verse may stand out: "And Jeremiah sang a lament [or laments] over Josiah. And all the male and female singers spoke of Josiah in their laments, unto this day. And they made them a fixed observance for Israel. And behold they are written in the [book of] Laments." Actually nothing in the extant book of Lamentations can be taken as referring to the death of Josiah in 609 B.C.E. The reference to the king in 4:20 must be to Zedekiah, who was king at the fall of Jerusalem. It is difficult to suppose that the Chronicler is simply mistaken, that he actually intended to ascribe authorship of the canonical book to Jeremiah. It is easier to suppose that he gives correct information: Jeremiah, and others as well, composed laments over Josiah, and these were gathered in a book called "Lamentations," but this has nothing directly to do with the extant biblical book. Nevertheless, the Chronicler's statement that Jeremiah wrote "laments" would have encouraged the idea that he was the author of Lamentations, especially because very early on some passages in the biblical book were taken to refer to Josiah (see the Targum on 1:18; 4:20).[9] To sum up, if one accepts the anonymous authorship of Lamentations, it is possible to give a plausible account of how it could have come to be ascribed to Jeremiah and eventually to be placed after the book of Jeremiah.

If one assumes the opposite, that the book was understood as

[9] The idea that Josiah is spoken of in 4:20 was picked up by Saint Jerome and from him by the *Glossa interlinearis*, and thence by later medieval commentators; see Ricciotti 1924: 32–34.

Jeremiah's from the beginning, it is difficult to suggest any good reason why it was ever separated from his other writings or circulated without his name. Wiesmann's argument (1954) that this was done for liturgical reasons, in order to group Lamentations with the other Scrolls, is without force, for the oldest listing of the Writings does not group the Scrolls together, and yet includes Lamentations (see above, "Place in the Canon").

In addition, there is evidence within the book that makes it difficult to suppose that Jeremiah wrote it. Certain statements would be, if not impossible, then at least out of character in the mouth of Jeremiah. For example, 4:17, with its pathetic description of how "we" looked in vain for help from "a nation that does not save," is at variance with Jeremiah's outspoken hostility to reliance on help from other nations (Jer 2:18), and the fact that he did not expect help from Egypt (37:5–10). Would Jeremiah, who prophesied the destruction of the temple, have written 1:10? The high hopes set on Zedekiah in 4:20 ("the breath of our nostrils . . . of whom we said, 'In his shadow we will live among the nations'") are not easy to square with Jeremiah's blunt words to the same king: "You will be given into the hand of the king of Babylon" (37:17). "Her prophets find no vision from the LORD" (2:9) is in the last analysis a rather odd statement from one who prophesied before, during, and after the catastrophe. If 4:19 refers to the flight of Zedekiah (see 2 Kgs 25:4–5) and implies that the author took part, as many suppose (see the COMMENT on the passage), then the author was not Jeremiah, who was in prison at the time (Jer 38:28). It may be granted that any of the above-mentioned details has seemed to some scholars compatible with authorship by Jeremiah, and that those who oppose it do not fully agree on which set of arguments proves the case! Even so, these and other details in the book suggest an author or authors more closely identified with the common hopes and fears of the people than it was possible for Jeremiah to be. This point seems to hold true even allowing for the requirements of the "City-Lament" genre (see below) and for the book's ritual purpose.

Arguments from the language of the book, especially from the vocabulary employed,[10] and from the acrostic form have been used

[10] The lexical evidence is exhaustively presented in Löhr 1894b; cf. idem, 1904 and 1905.

by those who wish to deny authorship to Jeremiah. These arguments seem indecisive. The lexical evidence seems to suggest that the book has ties with Ezekiel, Second Isaiah, the Psalms, and Jeremiah—that is, its vocabulary not surprisingly resembles that of roughly contemporary writers in some respects.

There is no conclusive evidence to indicate whether the book is the work of one author or of several, and both views have been defended in modern times. In this commentary, an attempt is made to read the poems, in the order in which they occur, as constituting a meaningful poetic unity.[11] Yet even if this meaningful sequence and unity of form is present—in itself debatable—it may have been achieved by one author or by several, and perhaps through an editorial process of considerable complexity. So as not always to be saying "author or authors," I regularly use the singular form in my NOTES and COMMENTS, without the intention of suggesting that we know in detail how the book came into being.

Some recent commentators, notably Gottwald (1962), Albrektson (1963), and Kraus (1968), have devoted effort to delineating the theological traditions on which the author drew, and on this basis have offered conjectures as to the circles from which the book must have come. In Kraus's opinion the author was apparently from among the cult prophets or the priesthood of Jerusalem, while according to Gottwald he unites the spirit of both priest and prophet, so that the book may offer evidence that there were indeed cult prophets in ancient Israel.[12] It seems possible that the author was

[11] Grossberg 1989 is an attempt to evaluate the degree of artistic integration in Lamentations. Grossberg finds the book "near the midpoint on the centripetal/centrifugal continuum" (p. 14) and says, "The work balances on the line between unity and diversity."

[12] Gilbert Brunet (1968) argues at length that the first four Lamentations were written by a (half-repentant) representative of the nationalist party, probably the high priest Seraiah, *against* the unpatriotic prophetic party of Jeremiah. The conclusions reached do not agree well with the relatively untendentious character of the book and are achieved only by a very strained exegesis, a main prop of the argument being that one must distinguish sharply between ṣar 'enemy' and 'ōyēb 'foe' throughout the book. Giorgio Buccellati (1960) argues from passages in Lamentations that the book comes from a party hostile to Gedaliah: a group of Jerusalemites who opposed his governing from Mizpah, of patriots who hated collaborators. The evidence cited is insufficient to render any of these conclusions probable.

14

an intellectual, a layman; and indeed it has often been supposed, on the basis of 4:19–20, that he was someone connected with the royal court.[13]

# PLACE OF COMPOSITION

The events and conditions with which the book of Lamentations deals are without exception located in Judah. This is subject to the qualification that much of the language of the book is universal and nonspecific. Yet at least one can assert that the book evinces no acquaintance with or special interest in the plight of exiles in Babylon or Egypt. In the absence of any strong evidence to the contrary, then, it seems best to suppose that the book was written in Palestine. Scholars have proposed that the whole book, or parts of it, were composed elsewhere, and it must be conceded that Jews in exile—Ezekiel is a notable example—could be very well informed about conditions back home; but nothing in the book furnishes positive evidence that it was written by an exile.

# LAMENTATIONS AS POETRY

## Introductory

Lamentations is all poetry. In its Hebrew form there appear elements corresponding rather closely to the identifying marks of some kinds of verse in our own language. Lamentations is poetry, then, not just in the sense that it is language out of the ordinary, full of imagery and memorable phrases, but in the sense that it is verse: that is, it is metrical. In it there is an extraordinary amount of repetition of lines of the same length and rhythmic type, and patterning of other kinds that we commonly associate with verse. In

---

[13] Tigay (1971) emphasizes the ties of the book, especially chap. 3, to the conception of the value of suffering found in OT Wisdom Literature, and sees a definite connection of Lamentations to royal circles and to Deuteronomy; such a view seems essentially in harmony with that presented here.

Hebrew verse, an important distinguishing mark is parallelism, which appears abundantly and in many forms in Lamentations.

The experienced reader who studies Lamentations in English, in this translation, or another, or several, will have no illusions that any version captures all of the poetry of the original, but perhaps will be encouraged by reflecting that much of this verse patterning does come through in translation. Especially the more conspicuous features survive the transfer to another language, like the contours of a body that can be seen—or felt—even though fully clothed. The following paragraphs point out some of these more conspicuous features; they also take in questions about the genre or genres represented in the book, and other matters of poetics. Here and there the translation and NOTES call attention to details of verse patterning. This much attention is devoted to poetics because the verse patterns are not the nutshell surrounding a kernel, a thing we can discard once it is cracked, but a set of clues—commands even —that indicate how we are to read the text, in its ancient literary context. In this author's view, by tradition and by design, the form of Lamentations was shaped to be consonant with the mourning, elegiac nature of the rites in which the poems were sung.

## Poetic Meter and Related Rhythmic Features

The writer of Lamentations chose for his poems a dominant meter highly suitable, by its phonetic qualities and by its associations, for the plaintive effect he sought. Such an assertion, in the face of the fact, acknowledged by all, that our knowledge of Hebrew meter is incomplete and that competing theories abound,[14]

---

[14] One major school of thought about Hebrew meter—the chief representatives being Hölscher, Mowinckel, Horst, and Segert—holds that the decisive characteristic of Hebrew meter (at least in the period we are concerned with) is alternation of stressed and unstressed syllables of the same length, much as in Syriac meter. See Hölscher 1920; Mowinckel 1950; Horst 1953; and Segert 1969, with references (n. 7) to his earlier studies. A more widely followed system has been that of Ley (1875) as modified by Sievers (1901–7) and subsequent students. In this system, the basis of Hebrew meter is not syllables, but accents. The various types of lines are distinguished by various numbers and patterns of accents. It is characteristic of followers of this school that rhythmic patterns are symbolized by numbers; thus a line made up of two parts (bicolon), each containing three ac-

requires explanation, justification, and some qualification. But, after reviewing some of the multitudinous complications that attend this subject, we will step outside the superabundance of trees for a moment, and will perhaps be able to see a forest.

**The Meter Used in Lamentations**   The acrostic form of the first four chapters permits us in most cases to divide the poems into lines as the author intended. Chapter 3 is especially valuable in this respect. It is partly due to this fortunate circumstance that Lamentations has occupied so prominent a place in the study of Hebrew meter. A more important factor, however, has been the recognition that these lines follow a rhythmic pattern that seems relatively easy to detect and to distinguish from other varieties of Hebrew verse: the so-called *qinah,* or "lament," meter.

The classic essay on the meter of Lamentations is Karl Budde's "Das hebräische Klagelied" (1882). According to Budde, the formal unit in Lamentations is a line divided into two parts by a break in sense. The first part of each line is a normal half line (colon) of Hebrew poetry, while the second part is shorter than the normal colon. This second half line cannot be only a single word, however, but must be a group of two or more words. Since the first half line must be at least one word longer, the lines are of the pattern 3 + 2, 4 + 3, 4 + 2, and so on. The numbers in these proportions refer to the number of major word-stresses in the half line. The effect is "a

---

cents, will be described as 3 + 3. Occasionally I follow the practice of referring to 2 + 2, etc., in the NOTES and COMMENTS below, without the intention of indicating adherence to the accentual theory. In recent years a different view has been advocated by David Noel Freedman, who describes lines of Hebrew verse according to the number of *syllables* per colon (part of a line) or bicolon, while the rhythmic pattern of syllables within the line, and the number of accents, are not treated as relevant. See his "Archaic Forms in Early Hebrew Poetry," ZAW 72 (1960): 101–7; "The Structure of Job 3," *Biblica* 49 (1968): 503–8; 1972a; 1972b; and 1986. On the whole subject, with extensive bibliography, see Wilfred G. E. Watson, *Classical Hebrew Poetry: A Guide to Its Techniques,* Journal for the Study of the Old Testament, Supplement Series 26 (Sheffield, 1984); for a brief and illuminating sketch, see Benjamin Hrushovski, "Note on the Systems of Hebrew Versification," in *The Penguin Book of Hebrew Verse,* ed. T. Carmi (Harmondsworth, 1981), 57–72.

peculiar limping rhythm, in which the second member as it were dies away and expires."[15]

Budde found this meter most readily evident in chapter 3, where apparent exceptions are, in his opinion, either indications of textual corruption or examples of some permissible variants to the normal pattern. For example, occasionally the first colon is shorter than the second, producing a 2 + 3 line; in such cases one must assume a tension between the artificial poetic rhythm and the actual, natural sentence rhythm. At the cost of somewhat greater effort he goes on to discover the same sort of unbalanced verse in all the lines of chapters 4, 1, and 2, without exception.

Budde further asserts that this type of verse is found elsewhere in the Bible also, and that the evidence suggests that it was the specific meter traditionally used for singing laments over the dead. He therefore titles it *qinah* meter, from the Hebrew word for a lament. (There is very general agreement that chapter 5 is in a different rhythm, being divided into cola of equal length, a pattern extremely common in the Old Testament.)

Since Budde wrote, Sievers especially has shown that in Lamentations a sizable proportion of the lines are not in Budde's unbalanced *qinah* meter, but consist of evenly balanced cola. Although scholars would disagree with details of Sievers's own analysis, as he himself anticipated, many would now be inclined to say that Budde overstated his case. Some lines are better described as 2 + 2 (e.g., 4:13a, b), and some are probably 3 + 3, though there is greater reluctance to recognize the latter type as legitimate, many scholars preferring to emend lines of this sort. Possible examples of 3 + 3 are 1:1a, 8a, 16a, 21b; 2:9a, 17c, 20a; 3:64, 66; 4:1a, 8b. Thus Budde's view must be modified by saying that the *qinah* line is at best the dominant line in Lamentations; other metric patterns occur more or less at random throughout the first four chapters. Atypical verses are especially common in chapter 1, and less so in chapter 3.

A second major qualification of Budde's theory is also of some importance: the dominant verse-type cannot properly be called *qinah* (lament) meter, because it is used in various classes of Hebrew poems having nothing to do with laments for the dead.

[15] Budde 1902: 5.

Sievers, one of the first to raise this objection, cites as other passages in this meter Isa 1:10–12 (a prophetic oracle of judgment); Isa 40:9ff. (an oracle of hope); Jonah 2:3–10 (= 2–9E; psalm of lament by an individual); Cant 1:9–11 (part of a love song), as well as others. Moreover, certain funeral songs are not in *qinah* meter, notably David's lament over Saul and Jonathan (2 Sam 1:17–27).[16]

**Parallelism and Syntax in Lamentations**  Study of parallelism in the poetry of Lamentations, and of certain characteristic syntactic peculiarities, adds several necessary preliminary qualifications to the general picture of meter in Lamentations.

Poetic parallelism may be illustrated by almost any verse from chapter 5 of Lamentations, for example, 5:2:

> Our property has gone to strangers;
> > Our houses, to foreigners.

The second colon corresponds to and resembles the first, that is, there is a semantic association between "property" and "houses" and between "strangers" and "foreigners," and in this case the verb of the first colon is to be understood also with the second even though it is not repeated. Such resemblance between poetic units is, as is well known, a pervasive feature of Hebrew poetry, and is found to some extent throughout Lamentations. But parallelism is not present in *all* lines of Lamentations. (By line I mean a line of Hebrew text as printed in the *Biblia hebraica Stuttgartensia*, which is a satisfactory working definition.) If we disregard what has traditionally been called "synthetic" parallelism, that is, cases in which a line may be separated into two parts but there is no clear semantic or grammatical resemblance between the two, 104 of the 266 lines in the book do not exhibit parallelism (39 percent). More significant is the contrast between chapter 5 and the first four chapters. There is a much higher proportion of parallelism in 5, where only three lines out of twenty-two (14 percent) do not have parallelism.

---

[16] The history of study of *qinah* meter is reviewed by W. Randall Garr (1983), with valuable advances of his own. Garr's study deliberately excludes the book of Lamentations, but asserts positively the existence of a distinctive *qinah* meter and its "choked or sobbing effect," referring to the description of Budde.

One may note that two of these lines, 5:9 and 10, while without internal parallelism, might be regarded as parallel to each other (external parallelism). By contrast, in the first four chapters 101 of 244 lines (41 percent) do not contain parallelism. This contrast amplifies the notion that chapter 5's poetic style differs from that of chapters 1–4, and that it is not solely a metrical difference.

Even though others would undoubtedly disagree with me concerning the presence or absence of parallelism in individual verses, the general pattern sketched above is probably correct. If so, the description of the meter is affected. I have described it above as consisting of *qinah* verse for the most part, that is, lines having a longer first colon, followed by a shorter second colon. Interspersed, it was said, are lines consisting of equal parts. When parallelism is obviously present, there is no difficulty with this description; for example, in 2:7, "The Lord rejected his own altar; he spurned his sanctuary," there is no problem in deciding what are the cola and where the division between them lies. But when parallelism is not present, the question of where to divide the verse becomes acute. Or is it correct to assume that the verse is divided at all? Budde, and others after him, speak of a division produced by a "break in sense," but this concept is vague, and in practice it seems that Budde and others have followed a kind of intuition when deciding where the caesura comes, instead of any rigorously defined principle. Lines without parallelism consist for the most part of a single sentence; thus, for example, 1:2b: *'ēn lāh mᵉnahēm mikkol 'ōhᵃbehā* (word for word: "There-is-not to-her a-comforter out-of-all her-lovers"). To make two parts out of these lines with only one sentence, it is necessary to divide at a great variety of places with respect to syntax: between nominal subject and verb in 1:1c; between a prepositional phrase modifying a verb and a following nominal subject, in 1:1b; between a nominal subject and a prepositional phrase modifying it, in 1:2b; between verb and prepositional phrase modifying it, in 1:3c—and so on through almost ever combination of sentence elements. To put it in another way, it seems impossible to define syntactically where the division between cola (caesura) is to be made in these lines. At least, no one has yet offered a satisfactory definition.[17] If one is to continue to describe these lines as made up

---

[17] J. Begrich (1933–34) asserts that the caesura cannot interrupt a construct chain or fall between the two accented syllables in a word with two accents;

of two cola, then probably it will be necessary to argue that the dominant pattern set up by the lines with parallelism shapes our reading of these lines.

Several further observations concerning the poetic style of Lamentations arise from studying the syntax of the verbal sentences in the book. Lamentations shows divergences from normal prose order of the elements that follow the verb in those sentences which contain a verb.[18] It is reasonable to propose as a hypothesis that metrical or rhythmic considerations have dictated this divergence from normal prose order where it takes place. Even if this claim is not obviously true, in individual cases (for example, 2:20c) these divergences may alert us to cases in which some element of the poetic line is given special prominence.[19]

**The Metrical Norm: Illusion and Reality** To step back now and look at the "forest," it is best not to make too much of departures in the book from the ideal metric pattern of a line consisting of long plus short. Second, the association of this meter with a particular set of circumstances or feelings—that of lament—may be genuine without being invariable or constant.

First, as to departures from the metrical norm, meter is, in our own poetic tradition, a matter of expectation, or even illusion, "created more by the mind of the reader than by the pen of the writer. . . . Only the hints and promptings are provided by the actual rhythm of the poetic words."[20] Whether from the way the writer prepares us in the first few lines, or from what we expect of a

---

obviously these restrictions still leave a great deal of room open. For a discussion of *qinah* meter and parallelism outside Lamentations, see Garr 1983.

[18] See Hillers 1974, with reference especially to works of Francis I. Andersen. Cf. Garr 1983.

[19] In this compressed account of the topic of syntax, one rhythmic peculiarity deserves special mention. In sentences with three postverbal modifiers, the poet shows a marked tendency to put the *longest* element last, regardless of its normal relative order. For example, in 2:6b it is syntactically unusual for the prepositional phrase to precede the nominal direct object: *šikkaḥ yahweh beṣiyyōn    mōʿēd wešabbāt* ("has-made-forgotten Yahweh in-Zion    festival and-sabbath"). But the compound direct object is very long as compared to the other modifiers in the sentence.

[20] Paul Fussell, *Poetic Meter and Poetic Form*, rev. ed. (New York, 1979), 15.

particular type of composition, we proceed through a poem impos-
ing a rhythmical order on what we encounter, or with the ideal
rhythm of the poem as a foil to the phonetic shape that is there. It
may even happen, as John Hollander's delightful work, *Rhyme's
Reason*, reminds us, that the meter of an English poem is not
announced by heavy thumps of the foot in the first line or two. The
first line may be ambiguous—he illustrates with a sonnet by Keats
—and the dominant meter of the poem may manifest itself only as
one proceeds farther into the composition.[21]

If, then, in Lamentations one finds apparent difficulty in a significant number of cases in reading a line as conforming to the
metrical norm, or if there is difficulty in defining where the break in
the line must come, in syntactic terms, the situation is not essentially different from that in English, and we may then more readily
accept the notion that the dominant pattern of unbalanced lines
justifies the reading of what we might call "undivided" lines as
consisting of a longer first member and shorter second member. We
need not be dismayed if the initial lines of chapter 1 or 2 or 4
present metric ambiguities. We may also readily think of lines consisting of a shorter member followed by a longer one as being deliberate departures from the common pattern, and need not suppose
that these in any way constitute a difficulty in thinking of Lamentations 1–4 as having been composed in *qinah* meter. Even a balanced line (4:13a, for example) may be at home in a poem of
dominantly *qinah* meter. We might best think that every line of the
poem diverges to some extent from the abstract ideal, but that the
book (i.e., chaps. 1–4) has, as an underlying structural control, a
single ideal metric pattern.

**Meter and Meaning**  Does the metrical form of Lamentations
itself contribute to the meaning of the work, by its association with
a tradition of laments? The *qinah* meter may alert us to a situation
in Hebrew literature like that which obtains with the English elegiac quatrain, also called the heroic quatrain. There is in our own

[21] John Hollander, *Rhyme's Reason: A Guide to English Verse* (New Haven
and London, 1981), 6–7. The line from Keats quoted is "How many bards gild the
lapses of time," which seems on first reading to announce dactyls; the remainder
of the sonnet is, however, in iambic pentameter.

literature, especially of a certain period, a stanza form (the *abab* iambic-pentameter quatrain) strongly (though not exclusively) associated with laments. The influence of a single composition, Gray's "Elegy Written in a Country Churchyard," has evidently been of great importance here, so that form has frequently been used in verse meant to convey, or parody, similar sentiments, those having to do with melancholy, loss, the mutability of human affairs—that "the paths of glory lead but to the grave." At the same time, the form is used for other purposes, and with other associations; hence the alternate name "heroic couplet."

We may then properly speak of this metrical pattern as "meaning" by association, in Fussell's way of putting the matter. When we turn to the Hebrew Bible, it seems to me that the evidence gathered by Budde is sufficient to connect the metric form of Lamentations to a tradition of laments, and that here we may think of the meter of the book as "meaning," that is, directing our responses to thoughts and emotions having to do with the genre.

We may also go farther in this search for the meaning of the metrical patterning of Lamentations, and look for ways in which the meter may "mean" by diverging from itself.[22] Words, ideas, and emotions may be brought into prominence by a departure from metrical expectation. We cannot expect to make refined and confident assertions in this matter to the extent that we can when reading poems in our own tongue. Yet we can perhaps in some cases, recognizing the limits imposed on us by the textual state of the book and our still imperfect knowledge of the meter, be more attentive to the possibility that there is interplay between the ideal meter of the book and the phonetic and syntactic actualities. With all caution, an example might be 2:14c, with which commentators and metrists have struggled. I would suggest that the unusually divided line focuses on and emphasizes the end portion, the compound object. For a different sort of effect, note 3:27, where a short first colon is emphasized, reinforcing the repeated "good!" with which each line of the stanza commences:

It is good for a man
    that he bear the yoke in his youth.

[22] Again, the term and thought follows Fussell, *Poetic Meter*, 12.

23

No attempt has been made in the present translation to reproduce or imitate the meter of the original. Occasionally a line, literally translated, falls into something like the typical *qinah* verse, for
example, 3:4:

> He wore out my flesh and skin;
> > he broke my bones.

**Strophic Patterns** The acrostic pattern in chapters 1–4 quite obviously divides these poems into units, which may for convenience
be called strophes or stanzas. In some cases these strophes corre-
spond to units of thought. Thus, for example, 1:2 presents a unified
picture—Zion weeps by night, forsaken by all her friends—quite
clearly separated from what goes before and follows after. In other
cases, however, the pattern marked off by the acrostic does not
coincide with the pattern of thought. Ideas and images may be run
on from one acrostic unit to the next. The last line of the *daleth*
strophe is 3:12, but the image of God as an archer is continued into
the first line of the *he* strophe, 3:13. This syncopation seems particularly common in chapter 3; see the COMMENT there.[23]

**Acrostic Form and Meaning** All five poems in Lamentations are
in one way or another shaped according to the Hebrew alphabet.
This is most noticeable in the first four poems, which are alphabetic acrostics. Chapters 1 and 2 are of a relatively simple type
in which each stanza has three lines, and only the first word of the
first line of each is made to conform to the alphabet, so that stanza
1 begins with *aleph,* stanza 2 with *beth,* and so on through the
twenty-two letters of the Hebrew alphabet. Chapter 4 is of the
same type, but here each stanza has only two lines. Chapter 3 is
more elaborate: each stanza has three lines, and all three lines are
made to begin with the proper letter, so that there are three lines
starting with *aleph,* three with *beth,* and so on. No attempt has
been made to reproduce this acrostic feature in the translation
given below, for obvious reasons, though the Hebrew letters listed
beside the stanzas are intended to call the reader's attention to this

---

[23] Grossberg (1989: 87–88) gives much attention to the "concatenation" of
stanzas as an integrating device.

phenomenon in the original. Ronald Knox did carry through the *tour de force* of reproducing the acrostic in his translation of the Bible, and a sample is quoted here (Lam 3:1–7) to give readers an idea of its effect:[24]

> Ah, what straits have I not known, under the avenging rod!
> Asked I for light, into deeper shadow the Lord's guidance led
>      me;
> Always upon me, none other, falls endlessly the blow.
> Broken this frame, under the wrinkled skin, the sunk flesh.
> Bitterness of despair fills my prospect, walled in on every side;
> Buried in darkness, and, like the dead, interminably.
> Closely he fences me in, . . .

Chapter 5 is not an acrostic, but has exactly twenty-two lines and thus conforms to the alphabet to a lesser degree. Other biblical poems with twenty-two lines exist—Psalms 33, 38, 103—and it is reasonable to suppose that in all of these cases the number of lines is chosen intentionally, though none is an acrostic.

Such a prominent feature deserves some explanation. After a survey of the meaning and functions of acrostics in general, and of the theories proposed previously for the significance of the Lamentations acrostics, I will present an additional suggestion, which may link the acrostic form of Lamentations 1–4 to the other metrical or rhythmic patterns with which it is interwoven.

There are many acrostic poems in the Bible and in other literature. Acrostic compositions were written in both ancient Egypt[25] and ancient Mesopotamia.[26] As is well known, the writing systems of these civilizations were not alphabetic, and therefore their acrostics are not alphabetic either. The most elaborate Mesopotamian acrostic is syllabic. The poem has twenty-seven stanzas of eleven lines each. Each line within an individual stanza begins with the same syllable, and taken together the initial syllables spell out a

---

[24] *The Holy Bible*, trans. Ronald Knox (London, 1955).

[25] Adolf Erman, *The Ancient Egyptians*, trans. A. M. Blackman (New York, 1943), lviii–lix, describes several compositions that, while not acrostic in the strictest sense, have the peculiarity that all of the stanzas have the same opening word.

[26] W. G. Lambert, *Babylonian Wisdom Literature* (Oxford, 1960), 67.

pious sentence: "I, Saggil-kinam-ubbib, the incantation priest, am adorant of the god and the king."[27] The date of this composition is uncertain, but is probably about 1000 B.C., earlier by far than any datable biblical acrostic. It has been common for scholars to minimize the possibility of a connection between biblical use of acrostics and these extrabiblical works, on the ground that these are syllable or word acrostics as opposed to the alphabetic acrostics inside the Bible, and that they are meaningfully connected with the sense of the poem, as opposed to the meaningless sequence of the letters in the alphabetic type. In spite of these differences, it seems that the basic idea of an acrostic, that is, of weaving a pattern of syllables or letters separate from its content into a composition at the beginning or end of the lines, came into Hebrew literature from outside. The major implication is that in discussing biblical acrostics we are apt to be dealing with a phenomenon that is quite ancient and far from its source.

Many explanations for the purpose of acrostics have been suggested, and there is no need to think that all served the same purpose. Especially in later times, in medieval magical and speculative works, ideas about the mystical power of the letters of the alphabet seem to have occasioned use of the acrostic form. A more prosaic purpose of acrostics was to aid the memory. Verse is easier to get by heart than prose, and still easier when the sequence of lines follows a set pattern. Finally, acrostics were written for what may be called artistic purposes: to display the author's skill, to make his work a more skillfully wrought offering to his god, and to contribute to the structure of the poem. Several writers have proposed that alphabetic acrostics convey the idea of completeness, that is, that "everything from A to Z" has been expressed.[28]

There is no reason to believe that the author of Lamentations or his contemporaries associated magical powers with the alphabet, as was done later. By the same token, although it is true that the acrostic form makes the poems easier to memorize, we have no way of knowing whether this was the author's conscious purpose, or simply an incidental effect. The suggestion that the book was deliberately written as a school exercise (so Munch) is extremely improb-

---

[27] Ibid., 63–68.
[28] Janssen 1956: 97; Gottwald 1962.

able. One purpose the author may have had in mind in choosing the acrostic form was to control and give form to the poems. The rigidity of the various acrostic schemes limits and shapes material that runs the risk of being monotonous and of lacking any clear progression of action or thought. In Lamentations, the impression is of a boundless grief, an overflowing emotion, the expression of which benefits from the limits imposed by a confining acrostic form, as it does from the rather tightly fixed metrical pattern.[29]

A further observable function of the acrostic form is to emphasize the *beginnings* of lines. In this it works together with a characteristic I will label "initial syntactic repetition" and with the unbalanced "lament" *(qinah)* meter to counter and check the natural forward and climactic movement of the lines of the poem.

**Initial Syntactic Repetition**   Repetition of the same grammatical forms at the beginnings of lines is employed with remarkable frequency in Lamentations. Initial repetitions of the kind I have in mind are not evident, at least not to me, in chapter 1. Chapter 2 provides numerous examples.[30] Note 2:10, where the requirements of English word-order obscure a striking sequence of "rhyming" verbs: "They sit. . . . They put. . . . They bow. . . ."

Initial repetition is still more prominent, and varied, in chapter 3.[31] In chapter 4 the initial repetitions are again less numerous and

[29] Bo Johnson, "Form and Message in Lamentations," ZAW 97 (1985): 58–73, makes the valid point that the acrostic form must be associated with the meaning of the book, but finds a structural significance for the acrostic quite different from that presented here.

[30] Thus 2a, b, c, 2:3a, b—five lines in a row—begin with first-person masc. sing. perfect verbs. After several pairs of the same sort of thing (2:7a, b; 2:8a, b), there is a still more striking sequence of three—or four—masc. pl. forms beginning at 2:10a (2:11a might be thought to continue the sequence). After some pairs of terms—thus successive lines with *māh* followed by first-person common sing. imperf. in 2:13a and b, and a pair of third-person common pl. perf. forms in 2:15a, b, followed by 2:16a, b, with third-person pl. perf. forms—we come to a sequence that begins in 2:18, either at c or possibly b (a difficult line textually) and runs through 2:19a, b, c, all with fem. sing. imperatives or the negative imperative.

[31] Thus 1, 2, 3 is an interesting alternation of first-person elements; 4, 5 follow hard thereon with verb forms that have the same grammatical form; soon we have the case of *gādar* repeated in 7 and 9; then three *waw*-consecutive forms in a row in 16, 17, 18; in 19 and 20 forms of the same root, *zkr*; 25, 26, 27 repetition of *ṭob*

striking, though a few occur: 4:5a, b; 7:a, b; 8:a, b (perhaps 16a, b also count).

**Acrostics and Word Order** There is another syntactic feature that calls attention to the beginnings of the lines. The acrostic itself does so, of course, but the little signal it gives, the bit of color at the start of the verse, is occasionally heightened if the acrostic word is out of place, that is, out of its normal syntactic spot, or otherwise odd. One could, of course, dismiss this as a bit of strain, a defect in the composition, but it is perhaps better to defer such a judgment and consider this phenomenon together with that of initial repetition. Thus 1:6 has the rather odd *waw*-consecutive form, but also an unusual word-order, with verb, adverb of place, then subject: "And has gone out—from Zion—all her splendor." Comparable are 1:15; 2:2a; 2:3a; 2:15a; 2:16a; 2:18a; and 2:21. Chapter 3 also seems to have noticeable divergences of this same kind from what is normal, highlighting the beginning: 3:2, 16, 17, 18, 22, 34, 35, and 36 seem slightly unusual syntactically; and in addition, in some of these cases, initial syntactic repetition occurs.

**Anticlimax** Complementing the attention paid by the poet to the beginning of a line is a tendency in some cases to an anticlimactic finish. Instead of the ringing finish, the end of the line may be occupied by words or phrases that for various reasons are not nearly as interesting as the more colorful beginnings. Thus we have lines that finish in unemphatic, flat adverbial phrases (2:1c; 1:12; 1:15a; 3:3). Stock phrases find a home in final position: thus compare 3:48 with 4:10b ("the ruin of my people"). Compare 1:16 and 1:9c, and other endings with reference to the enemy: 2:3b; 3:46; 3:52, or "there is none to comfort": 1:9b; 1:17a; 1:21.

To sum up, acrostic form is, in these poems, no mere ornament, and is certainly not a curiosity. Beyond its structural, shaping function, it combines with other features to make a kind of rhyme at the beginning of lines, using the term "rhyme" as a metaphor for a

---

with essentially the same syntax (assertion that the state of affairs is good); followed immediately by the repetition in 28, 29, 30; then 31, 32, 33 and 34, 35, 36; and in about the same fashion, slightly less concentrated to the end of the poem (43, 44; 53, 54; 55, 56; 58, 59, 60; 64, 65, 66).

metrical signal, a signal of an important node in a pattern. Not uniformly, but to an unusual extent, the reader's interest is drawn to what stands at the beginning of the line. And frequently the lines fall off, or die away, from the strong start, which reinforces the subtle effect of the truncated *qinah* meter.

The acrostic and associated features are most concentrated in chapter 3, so the book builds to a climax here. In chapter 4, the formal tension is relaxed, and, of course, in 5 there is a change into a different meter. If one thinks of Lamentations as a single composition, this arrangement can be viewed as appropriate and harmonious with the argument of the book, which also seems to reach a peak in chapter 3.[32] A nice detail may be observed in the last verse of chapter 4, where the emphasized initial word, the one that makes the last acrostic, is *tam* '(It) is complete'.

A minor peculiarity of the acrostics in chapters 2, 3, and 4 is that two of the letters of the Hebrew alphabet stand in the reverse of their normal order. Usually it is *'ayin* before *pe*, and this is the order in chapter 1, but in the other acrostics the sequence is reversed. This peculiarity is found also in the Greek version of Prov 31, and in the opinion of many scholars it should be restored in Ps 34, where the conventional order of the alphabet seems to violate the sense.[33] A common explanation, going back to Grotius, has been that the order of these letters of the alphabet was not yet fixed at this time. This hypothesis has seemed rather improbable in view of the consistent sequence *'ayin-pe* in Ugaritic abecedaries almost a millennium older than Lamentations, and in view of the order of the Greek alphabet, borrowed quite early from a Semitic alphabet. But in the recently published Qumran manuscript of Lamenta-

---

[32] Recently there have been renewed attempts to discover pattern and structure in Lamentations. See, for example, Johan Renkema (1988), who argues for a detailed structural pattern in Lamentations of a concentric type. One of his main conclusions, which is that Lamentations 3 is the center of aesthetic concentration in the book, around which other portions are organized, is in broad agreement with the point I try to make here, but the arguments he uses in favor of a detailed pattern of strophic arrangement and patterning of other sorts—including even *atbash*—seem to me unconvincing and strained. See also Grossberg 1989.

[33] See Paul W. Gaebelein, Jr., "Psalm 34 and Other Biblical Acrostics," in *Sopher Mahir: Northwest Semitic Studies presented to Stanislav Segert*, ed. E. M. Cook = *Maarav* 5–6 (1990): 127–43.

tions, 4QLam[a], this divergent order is found again in chap. 1, though it cannot be automatically assumed that this order represents the original reading, the author's intention. A very early ostracon containing the alphabet, published by Kochavi,[34] of about 1200 B.C.E., from a site in Judah, and abecedaries of about 800 B.C.E. from Kuntillet ʿAjrud in the southern Negeb[35] also have the order pe–ʿayin, and it has been supposed that in them and in Lamentations we have evidence of an authentic early Hebrew tradition of alphabetic order divergent from the Ugaritic and Phoenician order that became dominant. Naveh,[36] however, cautions that, at least in the earlier ostracon, the writing is unskilled in the extreme, and that in it there is another reversal of order (heth-zayin), which is simply a mistake by the schoolboy writer.

# Note on a Feature of Poetic Diction

Phrases of the pattern "daughter (Heb bat) X," or "virgin daughter (bᵉtūlat bat) X" occur twenty times in Lamentations, a remarkable number in so short a book, since such phrases occur only about forty-five times in all the rest of the Old Testament. Jeremiah has sixteen of these other occurrences, including eight occurrences of bat ʿammī (literally, "daughter of my people"), practically the only occurrence of the term outside Lamentations (the exception is Isa 22:4). It is reasonable to conclude that this poetic device was especially popular in the seventh and sixth centuries B.C.E., though it was no doubt very ancient, since Micah and Isaiah use it.

Lamentations uses bat ṣiyyōn 'daughter of Zion' seven times; bᵉtūlat bat ṣiyyōn once; bat ʿammī 'daughter of my people' five times; bat yᵉhūdāh 'daughter of Judah' twice; bᵉtūlat bat yᵉhūdāh once (these last two are not used elsewhere in the Bible); bat

[34] Kochavi 1977; see also Demsky 1977.

[35] Zeev Meshel, Kuntillet ʿAjrud—A Religious Centre from the Time of the Judaean Monarchy on the Border of Sinai, Israel Museum Catalogue 175 (Jerusalem, 1978).

[36] Joseph Naveh, "Some Considerations on the Ostracon from ʾIzbet Sartah," IEJ 28 (1978): 31–35.

*yerūšālaim* 'daughter of Jerusalem' twice, and *bat ʾedōm* 'daughter of Edom' once.

These phrases serve a poetic purpose in two ways. First, they help make explicit the personification of the people or city as a woman, and in this function maybe have a special role in the "city lament" (see below). Second, they seem to serve metrical purposes. The longer forms, the ones with three elements such as "virgin daughter Zion" are used to stretch out a name so as to make a whole poetic unit (colon) out of it. The shorter, two-part phrases such as "daughter Zion" seem also to serve metrical purposes, though these are not clearly definable in the present state of understanding of Hebrew metrics. The most easily observable pattern is that phrases of the type "daughter X" tend to stand last in the unit of parallelism (colon). This is true of all occurrences in the Bible, with a few exceptions (Jer 4:31; 6:26; 8:21; 51:33; Ps 137:8). There are practically no exceptions to this rule in Lamentations, the only possible case (4:3) being open to question textually (see the NOTE on that verse).

As has been observed by others, the renderings familiar from older English translations and the *Revised Standard Version (RSV)*, "Daughter *of* Zion," "virgin daughter *of* Zion," and the like, are potentially misleading, since the Hebrew phrases refer to the people or city as a whole, and not to a part of it. To put it another way, the relation between the two nouns in such a phrase is one of apposition; the second is not the possessor of the first. Since the main purpose of "daughter" and "virgin daughter" seems to be metrical, either other titles have been substituted ("lady"), or, in most cases, the title has been omitted in the present translation. Where a title has been omitted this fact is mentioned in the NOTES. This omission seemed advisable especially because no thoroughly idiomatic English equivalents are available. The *New Jewish Version (NJV)* uses "Fair Zion," "Fair Maiden Judah," "my poor people," and the like, which seem fairly close to the effect of the Hebrew. The *New Revised Standard Version (NRSV)* uses "daughter Zion," (1:6, etc.), "the virgin daughter Judah" (1:15), and similar renderings, for these repeated epithets.

# Lamentations and the City-Lament Tradition

Hermann Gunkel carried out an analysis of the five poems in Lamentations that has been very widely followed since his time. Chapter 5, he wrote, is a communal lament. Chapter 3 is an individual lament in the main, and chapters 1, 2, and 4 are funeral songs—not for individuals, of course, but political or national funeral songs.[37] As Gunkel himself stated, however, all but chapter 5 are mixed, impure specimens of the categories to which they belong: the individual lament in 3 is interrupted by a communal lament (vv 40–51). The funeral songs contain elements that do not properly belong there, such as the short prayers for help and the invocation of the name of Yahweh. In Gunkel's view, this admixture of alien elements is due to the relatively late date of Lamentations; the book comes from a time in which literary types are no longer kept separate, but are intermingled so thoroughly that even the dominant motif of a particular type may be lost.

It is evident that we derive relatively little help from such form-criticism for interpretation of the book. If one agrees, for example, that 1, 2, and 4 are funeral songs, one must immediately go on to note the fundamental differences from what is assumed to have been the classic form. Who is supposed to be dead? The question makes the difficulty evident at once, for the basic situation to which every genuine funeral song is directed is not dominant in these poems. And if, in its earlier portion especially, chapter 3 may be linked to the psalms of individual lament, the poem as a whole bursts the confines of this form. Only chapter 5 stays relatively close to the pattern of a traditional literary type, as defined by Old Testament form-criticism.

Since the 1950s, scholars have called attention to striking resemblances between passages in Lamentations and one kind of very ancient Near Eastern literature: the Sumerian laments over destroyed cities. When the biblical poet says of Zion, "She saw the heathen enter her sanctuary" (1:10), he echoes an old Mesopotamian plaint: "That enemy has caused men wearing shoes to enter

---

[37] Gunkel 1929. In his discussion of the funeral song, Gunkel draws on the study by Hedwig Jahnow (1923).

(my) cella. That enemy has brought the unwashed into the chamber. He has laid his hands on it and I am afraid."[38] "No one passes by; no one passes anyone else";[39] "The dancing places are filled with ghosts";[40] the fox who "droops his tail" in the ruined sanctuary[41]—such motifs from laments over ruined sanctuaries call to mind corresponding passages in the biblical text.

It is important for the student of the biblical book to have some explanation for these resemblances, not simply because it is an interesting question for the history of ancient literature, but because the biblical writer may have actually drawn on earlier, extrabiblical lament traditions. "Books are made out of other books," and, to the extent that this maxim is true, biblical books are no exception.

The Mesopotamian city-lament tradition is now more accessible to students of the Bible than before, thanks to a number of new editions and translations of the city-laments and their later continuants.[42] We have five Sumerian compositions ordinarily described as city-laments: over Ur; over Sumer and Ur; over Nippur; over Uruk; and over Eridu. A rather eccentric composition from this period, *The Curse of Agade*, is not a city lament but is related to the city-lament tradition in language and literary commonplaces.[43] The laments named above later became part of the curriculum of the Old Babylonian scribal schools. The same Old Babylonian period saw the creation of related kinds of laments, of which descendants or transformations were copied and used in liturgy down into the Se-

[38] From a lament translated by Mark E. Cohen, *The Canonical Lamentations of Ancient Mesopotamia*, vol. 2 (Potomac, Md., 1988), 721.

[39] Ibid., 331.

[40] Ibid., 336.

[41] A standard motif in the laments, going back to the third millennium B.C.E.; for examples see ibid., 113, 140f., 171, 268.

[42] W. C. Gwaltney conveniently lists the works published up to 1983 (see Gwaltney 1983), to which may be added Mark E. Cohen, *Sumerian Hymnology: The Eršemma*, Hebrew Union College Annual Supplement 2 (Cincinnati: HUC-Jewish Institute of Religion, 1981) and idem, *Canonical Lamentations*. Piotr Michalowski has issued a new edition of *The Lamentation over the Destruction of Sumer and Ur* (Winona Lake, Ind., 1989).

[43] Jerrold S. Cooper, *The Curse of Agade* (Baltimore and London, 1983). Note, however, that Michalowski, *The Lamentation*, raises important methodological and interpretive questions concerning the body of texts usually labeled "city laments" and their relation to the *Curse of Agade*.

leucid era. There are a good many Sumerian lamentations of late times with interlinear Akkadian translation.[44]

The repertoire of verbal parallels and parallels in imagery between the Mesopotamian texts and the biblical set of poems, already noted by scholars (among whom S. N. Kramer has been most prominent), has not been diminished by the new publications. A central and dominant image, that of the goddess who weeps over her destroyed sanctuary and ruined city, is fundamentally comparable to the personified Zion who weeps and is bewept in Lamentations.[45]

As an example, important for the following discussion, note one common city-lament theme, found in various compositions, with a parallel in Lam 4:5: "The king, who always ate fine food, receives (common) rations" (Lament over Sumer and Ur 305); "The . . . who ate bulls and sheep, lies (hungry) in the grass" (Lament over Sumer and Ur 313); these lines are in the translations and from the comparative table in Jerrold Cooper's *Curse of Agade*.[46] In the *Curse* itself, the commonplace appears in the form of a malediction: "May your aristocrats, who eat fine food, lie (hungry) in the grass!" (line 244).

The significance of these parallels is debated. Following the general line pioneered by S. N. Kramer, W. C. Gwaltney, Jr. has presented a definite answer to the question of the relation of the ultimately Sumerian material to the biblical book of Lamentations.

---

[44] See A. Leo Oppenheim, *Ancient Mesopotamia* (Chicago and London, 1964). Oppenheim also calls attention to the little lament over the destruction of Babylon in the fourth tablet of the Erra epic, which, in his words, "takes up an old Sumerian literary tradition, the lamentations over destroyed temples and cities" (p. 268). See Luigi Cagni, *The Poem of Erra*, Sources and Monographs on the Ancient Near East 1.3 (Malibu, Calif., 1977); the lament seems to be in tablet IV, lines 40–44, whereas the following lines may or may not be a continuation.

[45] An early study by Kramer is "Sumerian Literature and the Bible," in *Studia Biblica et Orientalia* 3: *Oriens Antiquus*, Analecta Biblica 12 Rome, 1959, see especially p. 201; a more recent study concerned specifically with the weeping female figure is idem, "A Sumerian Prototype of the Mater Dolorosa," *BA* (1983): 69–80; and see also earlier work, "BM 98396: A Sumerian Prototype of the Mater Dolorosa," *Eretz Israel* 16 (1982): 141–46, though Kramer does not in this case specifically cite Lamentations, confining himself to a reference to Jer 31:15, "Rachel weeping over her children."

[46] See above, n. 43.

In rebuttal of objections and doubts raised by others,[47] he argues that any "gap" that might have been thought to exist between a sixth-century biblical book and Sumerian city-laments of the third millennium has been closed by the publication of numerous later continuants of the old Mesopotamian tradition, and the proposal made by Gadd long ago is proved right: "the Babylonian Exile provided the opportunity for the Jewish clergy to encounter the laments."[48] Gwaltney proposes that, like Babylonian laments, Lamentations may have been used at the time of rebuilding the temple in Jerusalem, after the return. (For a reflex of this situation, one might compare Ezra 3:3, where weeping is associated with Zerubbabel's rebuilding.)

If one supposes, as I do, that the resemblances between the Mesopotamian laments and the biblical book of Lamentations are evidence of some kind of connection, an alternate view to that of Gwaltney might be considered by way of supplement or modification. Lamentations—a rather eccentric work, to judge from what has survived to us from ancient Israel—seems to draw also on the tradition of "laments of the individual" attested in the Psalms and on other currents of native Israelite literature, and yet another stream may feed into this work. We seem to have in the prophetic oracles concerning foreign nations, and also in those concerning Israel or Judah, indirect attestation of a city-lament tradition within Israel running as far back as the earliest prophetic writings, of the eighth century B.C.E. If so, any resemblances between the biblical book and Mesopotamian literature might point to earlier, even much earlier, contact between the two literary traditions.

Such a view might claim a kind of general a priori plausibility. The Israelites lived in a world of empires, city-states, and tribal groups whose ups and downs seem to have been of great interest to them, and of which they were evidently well informed. When

[47] The present writer, in the first edition of this commentary, expressed skepticism about any direct connection; cf. the study of T. F. McDaniel (1968a) and the judicious remarks of Tigay 1976: 140.

[48] Gwaltney 1983: 210. Note that Michalowski is pungently dismissive of the whole idea of comparing the biblical book to Sumerian laments. He refers (*The Lamentation*, 4, n. 24) to "the spurious attempts to connect the Sumerian 'city-laments,' with the biblical book of Lamentations." (The attempts, whether successful or not, are genuine enough.)

Amos says, "Go over to Calneh and see, and from there go to Hamath the Great" (6:2), he does not have to explain where these places are or what had happened. The question "Where is the king of Hamath? or the king of Arpad?" is rhetorical, presupposing a well-informed audience of frightened Jerusalemites for the Rabshakeh's taunt (Isa 37:13). Poetic treatments of world events in this rather small world, whether serious or mocking, may well have been cultivated in Israel and Judah, and also applied to the vicissitudes of their own cities and sanctuaries.

Investigation of the possible antecedents of Lamentations in Israelite literature has in the past been somewhat short-circuited by immediate invocation of the "funeral song" to cover cases in which a composition is labeled a *qinah* by the biblical writer or has prominent lament elements,[49] largely on the evidence of Jeremiah 9:16, 17 (= 17, 18E). Such a view remains popular, perhaps dominant or even general, today, to judge from standard commentaries.

To suppose there was a genre "city lament" in Israel, related doubtless to dirges over dead individuals but separate from the funeral dirge, might better account for some of the available evidence.[50] A "city-lament" genre would be an abstraction made, for the sake of discussion, to refer to a common theme: the destruction of city and sanctuary, with identifiable imagery specific to this theme and common subtopics and poetic devices. Influential model compositions closely embodying the ideal may have existed in Hebrew of the biblical period. If so, they have been lost to us, but what may be possible is the reconstruction of a dinosaur out of bits of fossil—if I am not constructing a Piltdown Man!

In the prophetic oracles, against Israel or foreign nations, are found rather close parallels to Lamentations, which have for the most part been noticed by commentators. These may reflect, however indirectly, a tradition of city laments. There follow some prophetic examples of lament language, often with parallels to Lamentations, which have elements that are not really at home in the funeral lament. I assume that the city-lament tradition, if it is really

---

[49] So Budde 1882; cf. Jahnow 1923.

[50] Appeal to the "collective lament" of the Psalter also seems not to provide a really satisfactory antecedent to Lamentations. (Examples of collective laments are Psalms 60; 74; 79; 80; 83; 85; 90; 137.)

reflected in prophetic texts, will be transformed somewhat or even parodied, for prophetic purposes. At this point I would recall the way in which the *Curse of Agade* borrows and parodies lament commonplaces.

Amos 5:2 and following is a famous passage, always cited in discussions of *qinah* meter and the funeral song.

> Fallen, not to rise again,
> > is the Virgin Israel;
> She is cast down on her land,
> > with none to raise her up.

This is in *qinah* (unbalanced) meter, and shares with Lamentations the personification of the people as a female figure, and the poetic title "Virgin Israel." The verb *nāpᵉlāh*, while one would not wish to press this detail, may well have the connotation "to fall in battle," or more generally, "to be slain by an enemy" (so Wolff),[51] so that the slain ends up stretched out on the ground. One may compare, as Wolff does, Lam 2:21. The "None to raise her up" of Amos is similar in pattern to a typical second (short) member of a line in Lamentations—thus 1:9, 17, 21. "Her land" is, significantly, a term for a nation's or city's territory; compare Amos 7:11, 17. Here, in contrast to the more general reference to lying on the ground, as in Lamentations, it is "*her* land, her territory."

The exploitation of a lament theme by Amos seems to continue in the next verse, 5:3, and is explicitly political or national, not personal in its terms. Decimation awaits Israel:

> The city that went out a thousand,
> > will have a hundred left;
> and the one that went out a hundred,
> > will have ten left.

The verse probably continues the little dirge begun in v 2, casting it in the future to make a prophetic threat, but keeping up meter and theme.

[51] Hans Walter Wolff, *Dodekapropheton 2: Joel und Amos*, Biblischer Kommentar 14.2 (Neukirchen-Vluyn, 1969).

Here we may have, in a tiny compass, early evidence for a city lament, or nation lament; if so, we would not need to resort to a tradition of funeral songs to explain its form and sense.

Here and there in Isaiah, especially in the oracles on foreign nations, one finds elements that may reflect a city-lament tradition. The passages can be only cited here, not discussed; the reader who studies them should look for the presence of lament elements— calls to weeping and the like—of images or commonplaces paralleled in Lamentations and elsewhere in laments, and note that in most of these cases the language is unlikely to derive from a tradition of individual funeral songs. Consult Isa 16:9–11; 15:5 ("My heart cries out for Moab"). It is striking that a good deal in Isaiah 15 could be read as a lament turned inside out, with description of weeping and mourning, the cries of the fugitives, and other descriptions of the ruin of the nation. This effect is heightened if one emends the difficult text of v 2 slightly, as has been suggested independently, to yield a sense "The daughter of Dibon has gone up to the high places to weep."[52] The female figure, personifying the city, weeps at the sanctuary. Compare also Isa 13:14ff.; Jer 31:15;[53] 48:17–18; 49:25–26. Jer 31:15 may be read in *qinah* meter, taking *qōl* (ordinarily a noun, "voice") as an interjection:

Hark!
In Ramah is heard a lament,
    bitter weeping:
Rachel weeping over her children,
    refusing comfort.

Note also Jer 48:17–18:

Console with him, all who live near him
    All you who know him by name!
Say: "Alas the strong rod is broken,
    The lordly staff!"
Descend from glory and sit in *thirst*(?)
    O inhabitant of Fair Dibon.

---

[52] See *BHS*, comparing Jer 48:18, as well as Syriac and Targum.
[53] Cited by Kramer in "A Sumerian Prototype."

Note these features: this is a lament, or mock lament; the meter is *qinah*; and a female mourning figure is present, who is referred to in the poetic manner common in Lamentations. Note too that the fictive dirge is put in the mouth of the neighbors: "All you who are round about him, and all who know his name."[54]

From such passages in earlier prophetic books, it seems to me not unreasonable to suppose that Lamentations draws on an ancient city-lament tradition within Israel, cultivated among "the male singers and the female singers" (2 Chr 35:25). In future, it may perhaps prove most fruitful to study the comparative question, that of connection to Mesopotamian laments, in this broader context, and not only in the setting of the Babylonian Exile.

# The Hebrew Text and Versions of Lamentations

## General

The Hebrew text of Lamentations is in a relatively good state of preservation, compared to the text of some other biblical books. This advantage in the commentator's favor is to some extent balanced by a corresponding disadvantage: the ancient translations offer relatively little help at those places in which the Masoretic text (MT)—that is, the received Hebrew text—may be suspected of being corrupt. Under these circumstances, commentators are compelled to rely to a greater degree on conjectural emendation of corrupt passages than might otherwise be necessary.

The textual evidence for the book of Lamentations has recently been enriched by publication of an extensive manuscript, one of the Dead Sea Scrolls, found in Cave 4 at Qumran, which has been

---

[54] Passages in Ezekiel also, chaps. 27 and 32, use the term "lament" (*qinah*) for hostile dirges directed, in hostility or mockery, against foreign peoples; some elements in these are not especially likely to have been in any funeral-song tradition, and may attest the persistence into exilic times of city-lament motifs.

given the official designation 4QLam[a].[55] This manuscript contains most of chapter 1 of the book. Aside from its intrinsic importance, the new manuscript helps set other scanty remains of Lamentations from Qumran, published earlier,[56] in a proper context, and assists in assessing the significance of some indirect textual evidence, from a small number of Dead Sea fragments that are not copies of the biblical books, but related compositions.[57] The Notes to the first chapter call attention to cases wherein variant readings from these various Dead Sea manuscripts merit discussion as possibly affecting the translation and understanding of the verse in question.

In the following paragraphs, under the heading "Excursus," I give a more extended general discussion of the textual history of Lamentations and of the nature of 4QLam[a] as a context in which individual variants may be studied. As a further convenience, a collation of 4QLam[a] with the Masoretic Text is given. Although these paragraphs are meant primarily to serve those who study Lamentations in Hebrew, other readers may find material of interest here. Each book of the Bible has its own history of transmission, differing in small or large ways from the fate that other parts of

[55] Frank Moore Cross, Jr., "Studies in the Structure of Hebrew Verse: The Prosody of Lamentations 1:1–22," *The Word of the Lord Shall Go Forth*, ed. Carol L. Meyers and M. O'Connor (Philadelphia, 1983), 129–55.

[56] These fragmentary manuscripts have the designations 3QLam[a], 5QLam[a], and 5QLam[b]. See M. Baillet, J. T. Milik, and R. de Vaux, *Les "Petites Grottes" de Qumrân*, Discoveries in the Judaean Desert of Jordan 3 (Oxford, 1962). Of these, 3QLam[a] is notable, not for any variant it contains, but because it is written (if the judgment of the editor is correct) giving respect to the poetic lines of the composition; that is, there is one poetic strophe (group of three lines of chap. 1) for each line of writing, instead of continuous writing. Like some other portions of Scripture, Lamentations was sometimes written "stichographically" in medieval manuscripts, that is, with special spacing that marked it off graphically from other biblical texts. This practice, the significance of which is debatable, is attested already in the way that certain other poetic passages are written in some biblical manuscripts among the Dead Sea Scrolls. For a detailed treatment, see James L. Kugel, *The Idea of Biblical Poetry* (New Haven and London, 1981), 119–27.

[57] The two noncanonical compositions referred to have the designations 4Q179 = 4QapLam, and 4Q501. See J. M. Allegro, with Arnold A. Anderson, *Qumran Cave 4*, Discoveries in the Judaean Desert of Jordan 5 (Oxford, 1968), 75–77; cf. J. Strugnell, "Notes en marge du volume V des 'Discoveries in the Judaean Desert of Jordan,' " *Revue de Qumrân* 7.26 (1970): 250–52. On 4Q179 = 4QapLam, see the discussions of Maurya P. Horgan (1973) and Hartmut Pabst (1978).

Scripture suffered as they went through the hands and minds of scribes.

# Excursus: Study of the Text of Lamentations and 4QLam^a

This new extensive text, 4QLam^a, is, in the description of the editor, inscribed in a Herodian script and hence dates somewhere between 30 B.C.E. and 70 C.E. It consists of three columns, containing Lam 1:1–17 and just the beginning of v 18, as well as a very small fragment of Lam 2:5.

The text is best approached in the context of the history of research on the text of Lamentations. Further, it seems good to assess the significance of the way that Lamentations was evidently used in worship and the way it was quoted and used in free composition at the time that the text was being formed. Lamentations was not just copied, from an old scroll to a new one; rather, it was recited, remembered, commented, used—and changed—by a living community. The Dead Sea fragments, taken together, may offer some fresh evidence for this process.

In connection with preparation of his commentary on Lamentations, Wilhelm Rudolph also published a detailed review of the Hebrew text and versions of the book, which is still of great usefulness.[58] More recently, Bertil Albrektson covered the same ground, with the notable addition of a detailed evaluation of the Syriac text of the book based on a new edition of the manuscripts.[59]

The conclusion that emerged from these studies is that in Lamentations the Masoretic Text itself seems to be in a good state of preservation, but that the ancient versions do not clear up many difficulties because they give a text not essentially different from the traditional Hebrew text. Since these scholarly studies appeared, new evidence and studies of the Greek text of Lamentations have shown that it belongs to the *kaige* recension, a kind of Greek text that has been brought into line, by ancient editors, with the emerg-

[58] Rudolph 1938.
[59] Albrektson 1963. Note also Gottlieb 1978.

ing received text.[60] To these textual studies one may add the recent work of Dominique Barthélemy, *Critique textuelle de l'Ancien Testament,* which contains a rich collection of evidence and opinion on difficult passages in Lamentations; most frequently Barthélemy and his collaborators defend the Masoretic Text.[61]

Among the Dead Sea Scrolls, until Cross's 1983 publication, we have had in our hands three fragmentary manuscripts of the biblical book. These new materials could scarcely change our general conception of the textual picture, as sketched above, because of their limited extent. The manuscripts are 3QLam[a], 5QLam[a], and 5QLam[b].[62]

In addition to these manuscripts of the biblical text, the Dead Sea Scrolls have yielded us at least two noncanonical compositions related more or less closely to Lamentations, 4Q179 = 4QapLam, and 4Q501.[63]

As an initial generalization about 4QLam[a], in the context of these earlier discussions and finds, we may note that it is not just an exemplar of the nascent or emerging Masoretic Text. Discounting the numerous sheer spelling variations (that is, mostly, *plene* instead of *defective* spelling),[64] and a case of variety of pronoun of a

[60] See Jean-Dominique Barthélemy, *Les Devanciers d'Aquila,* Vetus Testamentum Supplement 10 (Leiden, 1963), 33, 138–60; see also J. M. Grindel, "Another Characteristic of the Kaige Recension: *nṣḥ/nikos,*" *CBQ* 31 (1969): 499–513 (note that the LXX has *nikos* for *nṣḥ* at Lam 3:18 and 5:20). See also F. M. Cross, Jr., "The History of the Biblical Text in the Light of Discoveries in Judaean Desert," *HTR* 57 (1964): 283, and compare his latest judgment: "The Greek text of Lamentations is of relatively little use; it belongs to the *kaige* (Proto-Theodotionic) school which corrected to a Hebrew text of Proto-Rabbinic type" (Cross, "Studies in the Structure of Hebrew Verse," 136).

[61] Barthélemy 1986: 863–914.

[62] See references in n. 56 above.

[63] See references in n. 57 above. (4Q501 is both smaller in extent and less closely related to the biblical book, and, indeed, if the whole composition were known to us, might prove only to quote from the book.) Line 1 of 4Q501 rephrases Lam 5:2; line 5 has *hbyth wr'h*; line 6 echoes Lam 5:10 with [*nkmr*] *'wrnw wzl'wpwt* (cf. 1QH V 30). Less striking reminiscences—only possibly related to the biblical Lamentations—are *hšwmmym* of line 2, cf. Lam 1:16; 3:11; and *w'yn mšyb,* cf. Lam 5:21; Ezek 34:16.

[64] The collation shows such spelling variations at 1:2 (twice); 1:5; 1:6; 1:8; 1:10; 1:11; 1:13; 1:14 (twice); 1:15 (twice); 1:17, thus fourteen cases.

sort found elsewhere in the Scrolls;[65] and discounting also variants that are sheer scribal mistakes of dittography and omission,[66] and a few readings that in advance seem of the kind that are so minor and common as to be impossible to decide by any means but flipping a coin,[67] we are left—in the scope of the one preserved chapter—with a sizable number of variants from the Masoretic Text and from its close satellite in Lamentations, the Greek text.

This new manuscript may show signs of the use made of the book of Lamentations in worship, and in free composition as well. The compositions cited from among the Dead Sea Scrolls (4Q179 = 4QapLam; 4Q501) show us that Lamentations was not just copied, but used as the basis or source for free compositions. These works were evidently intended for devotion or worship, in their turn, at least in the broad sense that they are devotional or directed to God; they do not contain rubrics, but then neither does 4QLam³. 4QapLam imitates the style of the biblical book fairly closely, weaving in much other material; in it, as in the canonical work, there is an alternation of speakers. 4Q501 is, in the brief extent preserved, a prayer, being addressed to God throughout.

If we take just these fragments of compositions as a starting point, we gain some insight into the interpretive and liturgical context that surrounded this part of the biblical text in the Qumran community. The book of Lamentations existed under conditions that might be expected to have made it subject in special ways to the influence of one passage on another, to the influence of newly coined secondary material on the primary biblical text, and to what may be called modernization or smoothing or banalization—terms

[65] Thus 1:3 MT *hy'*]: 4QLam³ [*hy'*]*h*.

[66] The examples thus described by Cross seem to me to be correctly identified, though perhaps others could be added to the list, namely, the dittography of *lw'* at 1:6; the misdivision of *mṣ' wmr'h*, also in 1:6; and the rather long omission of the last phrase of v 10 and the beginning of v 11.

[67] There are a number of variants involving singular versus plural, or the interchange of the divine name (Tetragrammaton) with *'dny*, or similar small differences, which are also typical and common in medieval manuscripts, and whose textual merits or weight are ordinarily nearly impossible to decide. Thus 1:9 MT *'yn*]: 4QLam³ *w'yn*; MT *pl'ym*]: 4QLam³ *pl'wt*; 1:14 MT *bydy*]: 4QLam³ *byd* (note that Syriac here has singular *bida*); 1:14 MT *'dny*]: 4QLam³ *yhwh*; 1:18 MT *yhwh*]: 4QLam³ *'[dwny]*.

for the substitution of more recent linguistic forms for older ones, and elimination of uncommon and specifically poetic elements.

Similar forces for change affect the text of many biblical books, but in differing degrees and different ways. Since this is so, the liturgical character of Lamentations and the special place it occupied in the memories of the community are factors to be weighed along with more conventional text-critical considerations, and the new bits of Lamentations compositions may enable us to do more than make conjectures on this subject.

4QapLam illustrates the increased possibility of influence of one passage on another. The text shows that much material from Lamentations is being employed, but in an order and with new connections that break down the old connections that existed between lines in the biblical text.[68]

Newly coined secondary material may be illustrated by this from 4Q501 (1 line 1): *'l ttn lzrym nḥltnw wygy'nw lbny nkr* (literally, "Do not give to strangers our inheritance, or what we have worked for to foreigners"). Compare the canonical book (5:2): *nḥltnw nhpkh lzrym btynw lnkrym* (literally, "Our inheritance is turned over to strangers; our houses, to foreigners"). One notes how much of the biblical phrasing is retained, yet also the marked changes. Starting with the biblical line "Young children ask for bread; no one gives it to them" (4:4b), 4QapLam creates a new line: "They asked for water, but there was none to pour out [for them]."[69] Where the biblical text has only "the precious sons of Zion" (4:2, literally rendered), the writer of the noncanonical Qumran text creates a counterpart line "the tender daughters of Zion" (fragment 1, col. 2, line 13).

Also, in such compositions only loosely based on the biblical text, there was presumably less pressure on the writer to imitate exactly the older, more terse and poetic—and perhaps less well understood—language of the biblical model; he was free to modernize, and in the process to make his language more common-

---

[68] Thus, counting what seem to me obvious citations or allusions to the biblical book, I note this order of references in the preserved fragments: 5:16; 1:4; 5:2; 5:16; 4:3; 4:4; 4:5; 4:2; 1:1; 2:5 (or 2:7); 1:2.

[69] 4QapLam fragment 1 col. 2 line 8, translation of the (slightly) restored text by Horgan (1973).

place. This situation would have augmented the general tendency of copyists, consciously or subconsciously, to make the biblical text at hand more like the common language of their own time.

Turning from the noncanonical works to the new Qumran biblical text, we note that some of the variants of 4QLam$^a$ seem to show the influence of the interpretive context described above. One passage of the book influences another. Thus at 1:17, the words "Of all her lovers" (Heb *mkwl 'whbyh*) are added after "none to comfort her" (Heb *mnḥm lh*) under the influence of 1:2. This factor, the influence of one part of the book on another, is entwined in the complicated case of the strikingly different reading at 1:7 (see below).

Second, we may have the influence of newly coined material on the biblical text after which it was patterned.[70] In 4QLam$^a$ there may be such a case in the addition at 1:17 (see the NOTES).

Third, some variants of 4QLam$^a$ are the result of what may be called modernization, banalization, or smoothing. The substitution of the linguistically easier and modern for what is difficult and old is a phenomenon commonly observed in study of the transmission of ancient texts, and it has been amply noted in other Qumran scrolls.[71]

A special kind of banalization, more specific to Lamentations, is the loss of poetic perspective. The poems in Lamentations are not tightly organized, yet they do show signs of a careful, planned shifting of perspective. The speaker is sometimes the personified Zion, a female figure, then again a man ("I am the man," 3:1) who comes to speak for the community and personify it, and sometimes the community speaking in first person plural, "we." In the biblical book, there is shifting in the stance before God, from speaking of him in the third person to direct address. It is not all prayer to the deity. Such shifts take place within the single poem, chapter 1, which is the principal concern here. These poetic strategies are changed in the noncanonical compositions. The contemporary con-

---

[70] There seems to be an example of this type of influence also in 5QLam$^a$, one of the very small Dead Sea Lamentations manuscripts; see the discussion by Milik, on 5:3, in Baillet, Milik, and de Vaux, *Les "Petites grottes" de Qumrân*.

[71] Some possible examples in 4QLam$^a$ may occur at 1:6 (*bly kwḥ*); at 1:8; and at 1:14.

cerns of the community emerge more strongly. Thus in 4QapLam there is more of the first person plural, "we," and in 4Q501 those parts of Lamentations used are set in a direct prayer to God.

It seems to me that this kind of thing occurs, and rather pervasively, also in 4QLamᵃ. Thus at 1:11 the Masoretic Text has "LORD, look and consider how worthless I have become!" (r'h yhwh whbyṭh ky hyyty zwllh). In Hebrew there is a formal distinction between masculine adjectives and feminine adjectives. 4QLamᵃ substitutes a masculine form of the adjective "worthless," and the same thing happens twice in 1:13, where for the Masoretic Text's feminine adjectives we have in 4QLamᵃ masculine adjectives. The author has lost sight of the vividness of the personification of Zion as a female figure.[72]

4QLamᵃ also shows in places a shift away from the variety of the Masoretic Text to a stance of direct address to God, and to a preference for first-person plural forms for the community. For direct address, note 1:7, with its imperative "Remember!" This imperative is coupled with a first-person plural form, "our pain" (not in the MT).[73] For another change to first-person plural in 4QLamᵃ note 1:13, "And he brought us down" (wywrydnw, if indeed a final waw is to be read).

The preceding discussion is a kind of initial winnowing of the readings of 4QLamᵃ. The variants that remain—a substantial number—are not necessarily as good as, or superior to, the readings of the Masoretic Text, but they do call for individual consideration, and are dealt with in the NOTES. For convenience, the verses that contain the most interesting variants are simply listed here: (1) the order of vv 16 and 17 of chap. 1; (2) 1:7; (3) 1:8a; (4) 1:11b; (5) 1:12a; (6) 1:12c (hwgyrny); (7) 1:12c (ḥrwnw); (8) 1:14a; (9) 1:16a; (10) 1:17b; (11) 1:17c.[74]

---

[72] One may note that in this last case there is also a kind of shift from poetry to prose in the breakup of the syntax, where the addition of the Hebrew conjunction "and" (waw) shifts the construction of the whole verse.

[73] Compare the reading "our pain (mk'wbnw)" of 4QapLam, apparently corrected by the scribe to another first-person pl. form, part 1, col. I 14. In the opinion of Strugnell, Notes en marge, this was suggested by Mic 1:9, while the uncorrected text was influenced by Jer 30:15. In any case the suffix is first-person pl. "our."

[74] At 1:8b, 4QLamᵃ hzylw (without suffix) would deserve attention as a variant, but the reading of the first letters of the word is uncertain.

As a provisional summary judgment on the new manuscript, it does not, in the first place, line up with any particular known recension of this biblical book, neither with the Masoretic Text nor with anything in the Greek witnesses—hardly surprising in view of the textual history of Lamentations. Second, it shares many features of other Qumran manuscripts of the Scriptures and shows signs of being late and corrupt when taken in the context of other Lamentations materials from Qumran. Yet its variant readings serve to stimulate reconsideration of the Hebrew text at many points, and may also perhaps help us see more clearly where the Masoretic Text itself shows the influence of a community, studying and worshiping with an old book in a new age.

## Collation of 4QLam<sup>a</sup> with MT

Numbers refer to verses of chapter 1. The MT reading precedes the right bracket with a colon, which is followed by the reading of 4QLam<sup>a</sup>, according to Cross's edition. A question mark following a letter means that the letter is damaged but partially legible, according to Cross.

(2) MT *mkl*]: *m?kwl*; MT *'hbyh*]: *'w?hbyh?*

(3) MT *hy'*]: *[hy']h*

(5) MT *lr'š*]: *lr'wš?*

(6) MT (*ketib*) *mn bt* (*qere*) *mbt*]: *mbt*; MT *l'*]: *lw'? lw'*;
MT *mṣ'w mr'h*]: *mṣ' wmr'h*; MT *bl'*]: *bly*; MT *kh*]: *kwh*

(7) MT *zkrh*]: *zkw?rh*; MT *yrwšlm*]: *yhwh*; MT *ymy 'nyh wmrwdyh*]: lacking; MT *mḥmdyh*]: *mk'wbnw*; MT *lh r'wh*]: lacking; MT *ṣrym*]: *ṣryh*; MT *mšbth*]: *[kw]l mšbryh*

(8) MT *ḥṭ'*]: *ḥṭw'*; MT *lnydh*]: *lnwd*; MT *hzylwh*]: *h?z?y?lw*

(9) MT *pl'ym*]: *[p]l'wt*; MT *'yn*]: *w'yn*

(10) MT *l'*]: *lw'*; MT *yb'w*]: *ybw'w* (10–11) MT *bqhl lk kl 'mh n'nhym mbqšym lḥm ntnw*]: lacking

(11) MT (*ketib*) *mḥmwdyhm* (*qere*) *mḥmdyhm*]: *mḥmdyh*; MT *b'kl*]: *b'w?k?l*; MT *npš*]: *npšh*; MT *ky*]: *ky'*; MT *zwllh*]: *zwll*

(12) MT *'lykm kl*]: *'lyk [.]hkwl*; MT *'wll*]: *'wllw*; MT *hwgh*]: *hwgyrny*; MT *ḥrwn 'pw*]: *[ḥrw]nw*

(13) MT *wyrdnh*]: *wywrydnw*; MT *šmmh*]: *šwmm*; MT *kl*]: *kwl*; MT *dwh*]: *wd*[*w*]*y*

(14) MT *nśqd*]: *nqśrh*; MT *yśtrgw*]: *wyśtrg*; MT *'lw*]: *'wlw*; MT *khy*]: *kwḥ?y*; MT *'dny*]: *yhwh*; MT *bydy*]: *byd*; MT *l'*]: *lw'*; MT *qwm*]: *lqw?m?*

(15) MT *kl*]: *kwl*; MT *'byry*]: *'bydy* (apparently); MT *lšbr*]: *lšbwr*; MT *'dny*]: *yh?w?h* / /

1:17 (beginning with *pe*) comes before 1:16 (beginning with *'ayin*) in 4QLam[a] / /

(17) MT *lh*]: + *mkwl 'whbyh ṣdyq 'th yhwh*; MT *ṣwh*]: *ṣph*; MT *yhwh*]: *'dwny*; MT *ly'qb*]: *ly'qwb*; MT *yrwšlm*]: *ṣyw?n*; MT *lndh*]: *lndwḥ*; MT *bynyhm*]: *bnyhmh?*

(16) MT *'ny*]: lacking; MT *bwkyh*]: *bkw?*; MT *'yny 'yny*]: *'yny*; MT *mym*]: *dm'ty*; MT *ky*]: *ky'*; MT *npšy*]: *npš*

(18) MT *yhwh*]: *'[dwny]*

# SELECTED BIBLIOGRAPHY

◆

Fuller bibliographies of works on Lamentations will be found in the commentaries of Kraus (1968), Rudolph (1962), and Wiesmann (1954): the last named is especially valuable for its extensive listing of medieval works.

ACKROYD, PETER R.
1968
*Exile and Restoration: A Study of Hebrew Thought of the Sixth Century B.C.* Philadelphia.

ALBREKTSON, BERTIL
1963
*Studies in the Text and Theology of the Book of Lamentations.* Studia Theologica Lundensia 21. Lund.

BARTHÉLEMY, DOMINIQUE 1986
*Critique textuelle de l'Ancien Testament.* Vol. 2: *Isaïe, Jérémie, Lamentations.* Orbis biblicus et orientalis 50.2. Fribourg and Göttingen.

BEER, GEORG
1895
Klagelieder 5,9. ZAW 15: 285.

BEGRICH, JOACHIM
1932
Zur hebräischen Metrik. *ThR* 4: 67–89.

———
1933–34
Der Satzstil im Fünfer. ZS 9: 169–209.

BERGLER, SIEGFRIED
1977
Threni V—Nur ein alphabetisierendes Lied? Versuch einer Deutung. VT 27: 304–20.

BOEHMER, JULIUS
1908
Ein alphabetisch-akrostichisches Rätsel und ein Versuch es zu lösen. ZAW 28: 53–57.

BRANDSCHEIDT, RENATE 1983
*Gotteszorn und Menschenleid: Die Gerichtsklage des leidenden Gerechten in Klgl 3.* Trierer Theologische Studien 41. Trier.

# LAMENTATIONS

BRUNET, GILBERT
1968

*Les Lamentations contre Jérémie: Réinter-pretation des quatre premières lamentations.* Bibliothèque de l'École des Hautes Études, Section des Sciences Religieuses 75. Paris.

————
1969

Une Interpretation nouvelle du livre biblique des Lamentations. *RHR* 175: 115–17.

BUCCELLATI, GIORGIO
1960

Gli Israeliti di Palestina al tempo dell'esilio. *Bibbia e Oriente* 2: 199–209.

————
1961

In Lam. 2,5. *Bibbia e Oriente* 3: 37.

BUDDE, KARL
1882

Das hebräische Klagelied. *ZAW* 2: 1–52.

————
1898

Die Klagelieder. In *Die fünf Megillot.* Kurzer Hand-Commentar zum Alten Testament. Freiburg im Breisgau, Leipzig, and Tübingen.

————
1902

Poetry (Hebrew). In *A Dictionary of the Bible,* ed. James Hastings. Vol. 4, pp. 2–13. Edinburgh.

CANNON, WILLIAM WALTER 1924

The Authorship of Lamentations. *Biblioteca Sacra* 81: 42–58.

CARO, HERMANN ISAAK 1893

*Beiträge zur ältesten Exegese des Buches Threni mit besonderer Berücksichtigung des Midrasch und Targum.* Berlin.

COHEN, CHAYIM
1973

The "Widowed" City. *The Journal of the Ancient Near Eastern Society of Columbia University* 5: 75–81.

COHEN, SHAYE J. D.
1982

The Destruction: From Scripture to Midrash. *Prooftexts* 2: 18–39.

DAHOOD, MITCHELL
1978

New Readings in Lamentations. *Biblica* 59: 174–97.

DEMSKY, AARON
1977

A Proto-Canaanite Abecedary dating from the Period of the Judges and Its Implications for the History of the Alphabet. *Tel Aviv* 4: 14–27. Repr. in M. Kochavi et al., *Aphek-Antipatris 1974–1977: The Inscriptions.* Pp. 47–60. Tel Aviv, 1978.

DRIVER, G. R.
1934

Notes on the Text of "Lamentations." ZAW 52: 308–9.

————
1950

Hebrew Notes on "Song of Songs" and "Lamentations." In *Festschrift Alfred Bertholet*, ed. Walter Baumgartner et al. Tübingen.

EHRLICH, ARNOLD
1914

*Randglossen zur hebräischen Bibel.* Vol. 7. Leipzig.

EICHLER, ULRIKE
1978

Der klagende Jeremia. *TLZ* 103: 918–19.

EMERTON, J. A.
1967

The Meaning of 'abnē qōdeš in Lamentations 4:1. ZAW 79: 233–36.

EWALD, HEINRICH
1866

*Die Dichter des Alten Bundes.* Vol. 1.2: *Die Psalmen und die Klagelieder.* 3d ed. Göttingen.

FREEDMAN, DAVID
NOEL    1972a

Prolegomenon. In George Buchanan Gray, *The Forms of Hebrew Poetry.* The Library of Biblical Studies, ed. H. M. Orlinsky. Pp. vii–lvi. New York.

————
1972b

Acrostics and Metrics in Hebrew Poetry. *HTR* 65: 367–92.

————
1986

Acrostic Poems in the Hebrew Bible: Alphabetic and Otherwise. *CBQ* 48: 408–31.

FRIES, S. A.
1893

Parallele zwischen den Klageliedern Cap. IV, V und der Maccabäerzeit. ZAW 13: 110–24.

GADD, C. J.
1963

The Second Lamentation for Ur. In *Hebrew and Semitic Studies presented to Godfrey Rolles Driver*, ed. D. W. Thomas and W. D. McHardy. Pp. 59–71. Oxford.

GARR, W. RANDALL
1983

The Qinah: A Study of Poetic Meter, Syntax and Style. ZAW 95: 54–75.

GELIN, ALBERT
1951

*Jérémie—Les Lamentations—Le Livre de Baruch.* La Sainte Bible de Jérusalem. Paris.

————
1957

Lamentations (Livre des). *Dictionnaire de la Bible, Supplément.* Vol. 5, cols. 237–51. Paris.

GINSBERG, H. L.
1969

Introduction. In *The Five Megilloth and Jonah.* Philadelphia.

GORDIS, ROBERT
1933

A Note on Lam 2:13. *JTS* 34: 162–63.

———
1967

A Commentary on the Text of Lamentations. In *The Seventy-Fifth Anniversary Volume of the Jewish Quarterly Review*, ed. Abraham A. Neuman and Solomon Zeitlin. Pp. 267–86. Philadelphia.

———
1967–68

Commentary on the Text of Lamentations (Part Two). *JQR* n.s. 58: 14–33.

GOTTLIEB, HANS
1978

*A Study on the Text of Lamentations*. Acta Jutlandica 48, Theology Series 12. Århus.

GOTTWALD, NORMAN
K. 1962

*Studies in the Book of Lamentations*. Studies in Biblical Theology 14. Rev. ed. London.

———
1975

Review of D. R. Hillers, *Lamentations*. *JAAR* Supplement (June). Pp. 311–13.

GREEN, MARGARET
W. 1978

The Eridu Lament. *JCS* 30: 127–67.

GROSSBERG, DANIEL
1989

*Centripetal and Centrifugal Structures in Biblical Poetry*. Society of Biblical Literature Monograph Series 39. Atlanta.

GROSSFELD, BERNARD
1977

The Targum to Lam. 2:10. *JJS* 28: 60–64.

GUNKEL, HERMANN
1929

Klagelieder Jeremiae. In *Die Religion in Geschichte und Gegenwart*. 2d ed. Vol. 3, cols. 1049–52. Tübingen.

GWALTNEY, W. C.,
JR. 1983

The Biblical Book of Lamentations in the Context of Near Eastern Lament Literature. In *Scripture in Context II: More Essays on the Comparative Method*, ed. W. Hallo, J. Moyer, and L. Perdue. Pp. 191–211. Winona Lake, Ind.

HALLER, MAX
1940

*Die Klagelieder: Die fünf Megilloth*. Handbuch zum Alten Testament. Tübingen.

HELBERG, J. H.
1977

The Incomparable Sorrow of Zion in the Book of Lamentations. *OTWerkSuidA* 15: 27–36.

HILLERS, DELBERT R.
1972

*Lamentations*. Anchor Bible 7A. Garden City, N.Y.

———

Observations on Syntax and Meter in Lam-

| | |
|---|---|
| 1974 | entations. In A *Light unto My Path: Old Testament Studies in Honor of Jacob M. Myers*, ed. H. N. Bream, R. D. Heim, and C. A. Moore. Gettysburg Theological Studies 4. Pp. 265–70. Philadelphia. |
| HÖLSCHER, GUSTAV<br>1920 | Elemente arabischer, syrischer und hebräischer Metrik. BZAW 34. Pp. 93–101. Giessen. |
| HORGAN, MAURYA P.<br>1973 | A Lament over Jerusalem ("4Q179"). *Journal of Semitic Studies* 18: 222–34. |
| HORST, FRIEDRICH<br>1953 | Die Kennzeichen der hebräischen Poesie. *ThR* 21: 97–121. |
| JAHNOW, HEDWIG<br>1923 | *Das hebräische Leichenlied im Rahmen der Völkerdichtung.* BZAW 36. Giessen. |
| JANSSEN, ENNO<br>1956 | *Juda in der Exilszeit.* Forschungen zur Religion und Literatur des Alten und Neuen Testaments 69 (n.s. 51). Göttingen. |
| JOSEPH, MAX<br>1930 | Tisch'a Beaw. *Jüdisches Lexikon* 4.2. Berlin. |
| KAISER, OTTO<br>1982 | *Klagelieder.* Das Alte Testament Deutsch 16. 3d edition. Göttingen. |
| KEIL, CARL FRIEDRICH<br>1872 | *Der Prophet Jeremia und die Klagelieder.* Biblischer Commentar über das Alte Testament, ed. C. F. Keil and Franz Delitzsch. Leipzig. |
| KOCHAVI, MOSHE<br>1977 | An Ostracon of the Period of the Judges from 'Izbet Sartah. *Tel Aviv* 4: 1–13. Repr. in M. Kochavi et al., *Aphek-Antipatris 1974–1977: The Inscriptions.* Pp. 34–46. Tel Aviv, 1978. |
| KRAMER, S. N.<br>1955 | Lamentation over the Destruction of Ur. In *Ancient Near Eastern Texts Relating to the Old Testament*, ed. J. B. Pritchard. 2d ed. Pp. 455–63. Princeton. |
| ——<br>1969 | Lamentation over the Destruction of Sumer and Ur. In *ANET*, pp. 611–19. |
| KRAUS, HANS-JOACHIM<br>1959 | Klagelieder Jeremiä. In *Die Religion in Geschichte und Gegenwart.* 3d ed. Vol. 3, cols. 1627–29. Tübingen. |

—————
1968

*Klagelieder (Threni)*. Biblischer Kommentar. 3d ed. Neukirchen-Vluyn.

LACHS, SAMUEL
TOBIAS 1966–67

The Date of Lamentations. *JQR* n.s. 57: 46–56.

LANAHAN, W. F.
1974

The Speaking Voice in the Book of Lamentations (5:22). *JBL* 93: 41–49.

LEVINE, ÉTAN
1976

*The Aramaic Version of Lamentations*. New York.

LEY, JULIUS
1875

*Grundzüge des Rhythmus, des Vers- und Strophenbaues in der hebräischen Poesie.* Halle.

LÖ]HR, MAX
1891

*Die Klagelieder des Jeremias.* Göttingen.

—————
1893

*Die Klagelieder des Jeremia.* Handkommentar zum Alten Testament. Göttingen.

—————
1894a

Sind Thr. IV und V makkabäisch? ZAW 14: 51–59.

—————
1894b

Der Sprachgebrauch des Buches der Klagelieder. ZAW 14: 31–50.

—————
1904

Threni III. und die jeremianische Autorschaft des Buches der Klagelieder. ZAW 24: 1–16.

—————
1905

Alphabetische und alphabetisierende Lieder im Alten Testament. ZAW 25: 173–98.

—————
1923

*Die Klagelieder.* Die Heilige Schrift des Alten Testaments. 4th ed., rev. by A. Bertholet. Tübingen.

LOHFINK, NORBERT
1962

Enthielten die im Alten Testament bezeugten Klageriten eine Phase des Schweigens? VT 2: 260–77.

MALAMAT, ABRAHAM
1968

The Last Kings of Judah and the Fall of Jerusalem. *IEJ* 18: 137–56.

MARCUS, RALPH
1947

Alphabetic Acrostics in the Hellenistic and Roman Periods. *JNES* 6: 109–15.

MCCARTHY, CARMEL
1981

*The Tiqqune Sopherim and Other Theological Corrections in the Masoretic Text of the Old Testament.* Orbis Biblicus et Orientalis 36. Göttingen.

McDaniel, Thomas F. 1968a
The Alleged Sumerian Influence upon Lamentations. *VT* 18: 198–209.

——— 1968b
Philological Studies in Lamentations, I–II. *Biblica* 49: 27–53, 199–220.

Meek, Theophile J., and W. P. Merrill 1956
*The Book of Lamentations.* The Interpreter's Bible. Vol. 6, pp. 1–38. New York and Nashville, Tenn.

Meinhold, Johannes. 1895
Threni 2,13. ZAW 15: 286.

Mintz, Alan 1982
The Rhetoric of Lamentations and the Representation of Catastrophe. *Prooftexts* 2: 1–17.

Moore, Michael S. 1983
Human Suffering in Lamentations. *Revue biblique* 90: 534–55.

Mowinckel, Sigmund 1950
Zum Problem der hebräischen Metrik. In *Festschrift für Alfred Bertholet,* ed. Walter Baumgartner et al. Pp. 379–94. Tübingen.

Munch, P. A. 1936
Die alphabetische Akrostischie in der jüdischen Psalmendichtung. *Zeitschrift der deutschen morgenländischen Gesellschaft* 90: 703–10.

Oettli, Samuel 1889
Die Klagelieder. In *Kurzgefaszter Kommentar zu den heiligen Schriften Alten und Neuen Testaments,* ed. Hermann Strack and Otto Zöckler. Pp. 199–224. A: Altes Testament 7. Abteilung: Die poetischen Hagiographen. Nördlingen.

Pabst, Hartmut 1978
Eine Sammlung von Klagen in den Qumranfunden (4Q 179). In *Qumran: Sa Piété, sa théologie et son milieu.* BETL 46. Pp. 137–49. Paris and Louvain.

Paffrath, Tharsicius 1932
*Die Klagelieder.* Die Heilige Schrift des Alten Testaments 7.3, ed. Franz Feldmann and Heinrich Herkenne. Bonn.

Perles, Felix 1922
*Analekten zur Textkritik des Alten Testaments.* New ed. Leipzig.

Plöger, Otto 1969
*Die Klagelieder.* Handbuch zum Alten Testament 1st ser. 18. 2d ed. Tübingen.

Porteous, Norman
Jerusalem—Zion: The Growth of a Symbol.

W. 1961

In *Verbannung und Heimkehr* (Festschrift Rudolph), ed. Arnulf Kuschke. Pp. 235–52. Tübingen.

PRAETORIUS, FRANZ
1895

Threni I, 12. 14. II, 6. 13. ZAW 15: 143–46.

PREMINGER, ALEX, AND
EDWARD L. GREEN-
STEIN, EDS. 1986

*The Hebrew Bible in Literary Criticism.* Pp. 492–97 on Lamentations. New York.

PROVAN, IAIN W.
1990

Lamentations. In A *Dictionary of Biblical Interpretation*, ed. R. J. Coggins and J. L. Houlden. Pp. 382–83. London and Philadelphia.

RENKEMA, JOHAN
1988

The Literary Structure of Lamentations. In *The Structural Analysis of Biblical and Canaanite Poetry*, ed. W. van der Meer and J. C. de Moor. *Journal for the Study of the Old Testament* Supplement Series 74. Pp. 294–320, 321–46, 347–60, 361–96. Sheffield.

RICCIOTTI, GIUSEPPE
1924

*Le Lamentazioni de Geremia.* Turin and Rome.

ROBINSON, THEODORE
H. 1933

Notes on the Text of Lamentations. ZAW 51: 255–59.

⸻
1934

Once More on the Text of Lamentations. ZAW 52: 309–10.

⸻
1936

Anacrusis in Hebrew Poetry. In *Werden und Wesen des Alten Testaments.* BZAW 66. Pp. 37–40. Giessen.

RUDOLPH, WILHELM
1938

Der Text der Klagelieder. ZAW 56: 101–22.

⸻
1962

*Das Buch Ruth—Das Hohe Lied—Die Klagelieder.* Kommentar zum Alten Testament 17. 1–3. Gütersloh.

SEGERT, STANISLAV
1965

Zur literarischen Form und Funktion der fünf Megilloth (Im margine der neuesten Kommentare). *Archiv Orientální* 33: 451–62.

⸻
1969

Versbau und Sprachbau in der althebräischen Poesie. *Mitteilungen des Instituts für Orientforschung* 15: 312–21.

# SELECTED BIBLIOGRAPHY

SHEA, W. H.
1979
The *qinah* Structure of the Book of Lamentations. *Biblica* 60: 103–7.

SIEVERS, EDUARD
1901–7
*Metrische Studien.* 3 vols. Leipzig.

TIGAY, JEFFREY
1971
Lamentations, Book of. In *Encyclopaedia Judaica.* Vol. 10, pp. 1368–75. Jerusalem.

————
1976
Review of D. R. Hillers, *Lamentations. JNES* 35: 140–43.

WEISER, ARTUR
1962
*Klagelieder.* Das Alte Testament Deutsch 16. Pp. 297–370. Göttingen.

WESTERMANN, CLAUS
1954
Struktur und Geschichte der Klage im Alten Testament. ZAW 66: 44–80.

————
1989
Lamentations. Trans. by Bernhard W. Anderson. In *The Books of the Bible.* Vol. 1: *The Old Testament/The Hebrew Bible.* Pp. 303–18. New York.

WIESMANN, HERMANN
1926a
Der planmäszige Aufbau der Klagelieder des Jeremias. *Biblica* 7: 146–61.

————
1926b
Der Zweck der Klagelieder des Jeremias. *Biblica* 7: 412–28.

————
1927
Die Textgestalt des 5. Kapitels der Klagelieder. *Biblica* 8: 339–47.

————
1936
Der Verfasser des Büchleins der Klagelieder ein Augenzeuge der behandelten Ereignisse? *Biblica* 17: 71–84.

————
1954
*Die Klagelieder.* Frankfurt am Main.

ZENNER, P. J. K.
1904
Thr 5. *Biblische Zeitschrift* o.s. 2: 370–72.

ZIEGLER, JOSEPH
1976
*Jeremias. Baruch. Threni. Epistula Jeremiae.* 2d ed. Göttingen.

*4QLamᵃ (Israel Antiquities Authority)*

# LAMENTATIONS

◆

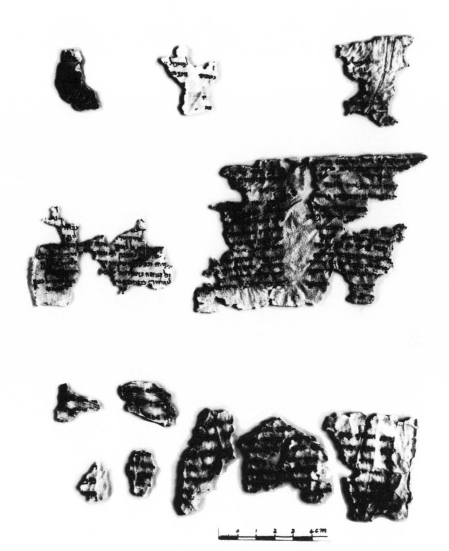

4Q179 (Israel Antiquities Authority)

"Is there any pain like my pain?"
(1:1–22)

aleph    1:1 How deserted lies the city    that once was full of people!
The greatest among nations    is now like a widow;
The noblest of states    is set to forced labor.

beth    2 By night she weeps aloud,    tears on her cheeks.
There is no one to comfort her    of all her lovers.
All her friends have betrayed her,    have become her enemies.

gimel    3 Judah has gone into exile    after suffering and after much toil.
She dwelled among the nations    but found no rest.
All who pursued her cornered her    in narrow straits.

daleth    4 The roads to Zion mourn,    since none come in for the feasts.
All her gates are desolate.    Her priests sigh,
Her young women are troubled,    and she is bitter.

he    5 Her enemies are now supreme;    her foes, at ease,
Since the LORD afflicted her    for her many rebellions.
Her children were driven as prisoners    before the enemy.

waw    6 And there has departed from Zion    all her splendor.
Her princes were like stags    which find no pasture,
But go on exhausted    before the hunter.

zayin    7 Jerusalem calls to mind    the days when she was banished in misery,

. . . . . . . . . . . . . . . . . . . . . . . . . . . . .

When her people fell into the enemy's grasp    and there was no one to help.

Her enemies saw her. They laughed    at her collapse.

*heth*    8 Because Jerusalem sinned so great a sin,    people shake their heads at her.

All who once respected her, despise her,    having seen her naked.

She herself groans aloud,    and falls back frustrated.

*teth*    9 Her pollution has fouled her skirts.    She did not think of her future.

And she has come down astonishingly,    with no one to comfort her.

"O LORD, look upon my misery,    at the insolence of the enemy!"

*yod*    10 The enemy stretched out his hand    after all her precious things.

She saw the heathen    enter her sanctuary,

Concerning whom you had commanded:

"They shall not enter your assembly."

*kaph*    11 All her people are groaning,    seeking food.

They gave their darlings for food,    to keep alive.

"O LORD, look and consider    how worthless I have become!

*lamed*    12 Come, all you who pass by on the road, consider and see:

Is there any pain like my pain    —that which he caused me,

Which the LORD inflicted on me    on the day of his anger?

*mem*    13 From on high he sent fire    and sank it into my bones.

He stretched a net for my feet;    he turned me back.

He made me desolate,    sick all day long.

*nun*    14 Watch is kept over my steps.    They are entangled by his hand.

His yoke is on my neck.    He has brought my strength low.

The Lord has given me up    to those whom I
    cannot resist.

*samekh*    15 The Lord heaped up in my midst    all my strong
    men,
    Then summoned an assembly against me    to
    crush my young warriors.
    The Lord trod the wine press    of the young lady
    Judah.

*ayin*    16 Over these things I weep;    my eyes run with
    tears.
    For any comforter, anyone to console,    is far
    from me.
    My children are desolate    because the enemy
    has prevailed."

*pe*    17 Zion spread out her hands    — there was none to
    comfort her.
    The LORD commanded Jacob's enemies    to
    gather around him.
    Jerusalem has become    like an unclean thing in
    their midst.

*sade*    18 "The LORD is in the right,    for I disobeyed his
    command.
    Listen, all you peoples,    and see my pain!
    My young men and women    have been taken
    prisoner.

*qof*    19 I called for my lovers,    but they deceived me.
    My priests and my elders    expired in the city
    While seeking food    to keep alive.

*resh*    20 LORD, see how I am in anguish!    My bowels
    churn.
    My heart is turned over inside me,    because I
    was very rebellious.
    Outside the sword killed my children;    inside, it
    was famine.

*shin*    21 Listen to how I groan!    There is no one to
    comfort me.
    All my enemies heard of my trouble; they
    rejoiced    that you had done it.

Oh bring on the day you proclaimed,      and let
them be like me!

taw      22 Let all their wickedness come before you,      and
do to them
What you did to me      for all my rebellions.
For many are my groans,      and my heart is
sick."

# NOTES

1 Before 1:1 of the MT, the LXX has this preface: "And it came to
pass after Israel had been taken captive and Jerusalem had been
laid waste, Jeremiah sat weeping and lamented this lament over
Jerusalem, and said——." The Vg also contains this prologue, in
nearly identical form. Although it is a later addition to the text,
based on the identification of Jeremiah as author of the book, note
that the style is Hebraic rather than Greek. Either it was translated
from a Hebrew *Vorlage*, or the author imitated the style of biblical
Greek.

1. *once was full of people!* For a line of strikingly similar construction and thought pattern, contrasting a glorious past with the
wretched present, cf. Isa 1:21: "How she has become a whore, the
faithful city!" On *rabbātī ʿām* as "full of people," cf. 1 Sam 2:5,
*rabbat bānīm* 'having many sons'. These parallels seem to make the
traditional understanding preferable to the otherwise attractive suggestion of T. McDaniel (1968b: 29–31) that, in view of the Phoenician and Ugaritic divine title *rbt*, one should render *rabbātī* in the
first and second lines as "The Mistress of the people . . . the
Mistress among the nations." This destroys the contrast with *bādād*
in the first half line; moreover, the extrabiblical parallels are not
exact. One could better think of the initial *rabbātī* as ambiguous. As
suggested to me by D. N. Freedman, the first colon, with its collo-
cation of *yāšab* and *bādad*, is ironic. Although the initial *ʾēkāh*
signals that we must understand *yāšĕbāh bādad* as a reference to
present misery, this combination of verb and noun (or with a se-
mantically related verb, *šākan*) is used elsewhere (see Jer 49:31;
Deut 33:28) to express, not loneliness and desertion, but solitary
security.

The epithets in lines 1b and 1c consist of a noun modified by another noun with the preposition *b*, and hence contrast with the construct chain of line 1a (*rabbātī ʿām*). The question is: What is meant by this *b*? It could mean "over" or "among." (Rudolph 1962 renders the first as "among" [*unter*] and the second as "over" [*Fürstin über die Gaue*], but it seems better to attempt to render it in the same way in both lines, because of the very close parallelism.) The translation "over" has often been preferred, especially for *śārātī bammᵉdīnōt* 'princess over provinces'. The masculine title *śar* (the feminine is of infrequent occurrence) regularly stands in construct before the thing ruled: note, for example, *śārē hammᵉdīnōt*, 1 Kgs 20:14, 15, 17, 19; Esth 8:9; 9:3. (Exceptions are only apparent; in Ps 45:17 [= 16E], *b* after *śārīm* is distributive, local: "princes *throughout* the whole land"; similarly 1 Chr 12:22 [= 21E], *śārīm baṣṣābāʾ* is "officers *in* the army," not "over the [whole] army".) In favor of "among," note that expressions like "great among (*b*) nations" are good Hebrew equivalents for the superlative. The preposition *b* is used in this way in Jer 49:15; Prov 30:30; and other examples cited in BDB, s.v. *b*, S 2a. Note that a Qumran composition incorporating citations from Lamentations— 4Q179, fragment 2, line 5—paraphrases with *śrty kl lʾwm[ym]*. If translated as is done here, lines 1b and 1c imply that the poet is not limiting the picture strictly to the "city," but has the whole state in mind: elsewhere also the poem occasionally has a wider perspective in view; note "Judah" in v 3; "Jacob" in v 17.

The sequence *rbty . . . śrty* in this verse is tantalizingly similar to a pair of Ugaritic adjectives, the standard epithets following names of cities: *ʾudm* (a city name) *rbt* || *ʾudm ṯrrt* (the first adjective means "great"; meaning of the second is uncertain). One may perhaps think of a reinterpretation within Hebrew poetic tradition of a pair of words that had become partly obscure over the centuries. Note that Heb *rabbāh* follows the names of cities in *ṣīdōn rabbāh*, Josh 11:8, and *ḥᵃmat rabbah*, Amos 6:2. The attempt by Jonas C. Greenfield to connect these Northwest Semitic epithets with Akk *šarratu* 'queen' seems to encounter a serious orthographic difficulty (why would an Akkadian loanword be spelled with two *r*'s in Ugaritic?) and involves an improbable phonetic correspondence; see his "The Epithets *rbt* || *ṯrrt* in the KRT Epic," in *Perspectives on Language and Text*, ed. E. W. Conrad and E. G. Newing (Winona

Lake, Ind., 1987), 35–37. Gene M. Schramm, "Poetic Patterning in Biblical Hebrew," in *Michigan Oriental Studies in Honor of George G. Cameron*, ed. L. Orlin (Ann Arbor, 1976), 180 offers a syntactic and poetic analysis of 1:1 that differs notably from the more conventional understanding reflected in the present translation and discussion.

2. A detail in 2a illustrates how late biblical poetry retained but modified age-old poetic tradition. The verbs *bākāh* 'weep' and *dāmaʿ* 'shed tears' are commonly used parallel to each other already in Ugaritic poetry, *bākāh* always in the first half line (or colon, to use more convenient terminology). That is to say, in the useful terms introduced by M. Held, *bākāh* is A-word to *dāmaʿ* as B-word (cf. Jer 13:17). Here also the verb *bākāh* is used first, but instead of a parallel verb there is a verbless sentence with the noun *dimʿāh* 'tears' as subject.

3. Although some versions and commentators have taken *min* 'from' here as causal, "on account of" (cf. Isa 5:13, *gālāh ʿammī mibbᵉlī dāʿat*) this reading is very strained in the present case, and involves the necessity of taking *gālāh* in a sense, "to migrate (voluntarily)," which it does not really have, in spite of Ezek 12:3 and 2 Sam 15:19, which are often cited for this sense. Hence the preposition must be taken to mean "out of" or in a temporal sense "after." The idea is that the actual catastrophe came after a long period of inglorious trouble and toil. Moreover, as Rudolph (1962) has argued with special persuasiveness, the remainder of the verse also refers to Judah's troubles *before* the captivity. "She dwelled among the nations" means "she was once an independent nation among the nations of the earth." Many commentators have thought otherwise (see R. B. Salters, "Lamentations 1:3: Light from the History of Exegesis," in *A Word in Season*, ed. J. D. Martin and P. R. Davies, Journal for the Study of the Old Testament, Supplement Series 42 [Sheffield, 1986], 73–89 for an extensive review of opinion, and a conclusion different from that drawn here), and indeed the line by itself could also refer to the scattering of the Jews "among the nations" following the fall of Jerusalem, which is often mentioned in the OT, and in Lam 2:9 as well ("among the heathen"). Since the combination of the verb *yāšab* 'to dwell' with "among the nations" does not occur elsewhere, it is especially difficult to decide between the two interpretations, but

the view that this is a reference to preexilic conditions seems preferable as being more in harmony with the whole chapter, which is not otherwise concerned with the plight of the exiles among the heathen. Note the close parallel to the sentiment of 4:20: "In his shadow we will *live among the nations*," an unambiguous reference to the preexilic period of independent nationhood.

*cornered her in narrow straits.* Literally, "overtook her between the narrow places." Since the Hebrew phrase *bēn hammᵉṣārīm* is unparalleled, the exact sense is uncertain. A "Thanksgiving Psalm" from Qumran (Hodayoth [1QH v 29]) paraphrases this line and adds, "so I could not get away."

4. *desolate.* To *šōmēmīn*, with plural in *-īn*, cf. *tannīn* in 4:3. *troubled.* The odd form *nūgōt* is probably best explained as a *niphʿal* participle of *yāgāh*; so most commentators, cf. G. Bergsträsser, *Hebräische Grammatik*, 2d ed. (Leipzig, 1929), para. 26g. The LXX's "led away," even if genuine and not due to inner-Greek corruption (so Albrektson 1963; cf. Barthélemy 1986), is not a good parallel to "sigh" in the second colon; note, however, Nah 2:8 [ = 7E]. To 4a compare "Lamentation over the Destruction of Sumer and Ur," *ANET*, p. 612, line 39: "That no one tread the highways, that no one seek out the roads." This is part of a curse pronounced by Utu (line 26). Cf. also Isa 33:8; Judg 5:6.

5. *are now supreme.* Literally, "have become the head"; see the COMMENT below.

*at ease.* The correctness of MT *šālū* is demonstrated (against Ehrlich 1914) by use of this verb in a similar context in Jer 12:1.

6. "And" at the beginning of this verse is rather awkward, since the connection to the preceding line is not very close, and since in good Hebrew poetic style one does not begin new lines with "and," to say nothing of new stanzas. In the present case, this is an artificiality into which the author was led by the acrostic. Because there are practically no other words in Hebrew beginning with *w*, the sixth letter of the alphabet, he must use the conjunction *w* ("and") here and in 2:6; 3:16–18; 4:6. Aside from these six occurrences, where choice of the verb form has been dictated by the acrostic, the writer of Lamentations uses *waw*-consecutive with the imperfect twenty-three times. This kind of form is not characteristic of archaic Hebrew poetic style, but the quantity of such forms in Lamentations is a sufficient indication that style has changed in this

respect by the sixth century B.C.E. (Note that with no real exception the LXX supports the MT with respect to *waw*-consecutives.) *waw*-consecutive forms tend to occur in just two poetic situations, a characteristic not easily reflected in translation. Of the twenty-three, seven occur at the beginning of the final line of a three-line stanza (1:6c; 2:3c, 5c, 6c, 8c, 14c, 17c) and one (4:11b) at the head of the final line of a two-line stanza. The other characteristic use is in a line such as 2:15b, where two verbs occur in the first colon in the line, and the second is a *waw*-consecutive form. This style of line is most common as the middle line of three (five times: 2:15b, 16b; 3:2, 5, 11), and it occurs just once as the first of three lines (3:43) and once as the third line (3:12). Aside from these two characteristic uses, *waw*-consecutive forms are decidedly unusual. Anomalous occurrences in 1:9b, 13a, and 2:4b may point to textual problems. A special case is 3:37, the *waw*-consecutive being in what amounts to a quotation (see the NOTE there). There remain four cases (1:8c; 3:33, 53; 4:11) that are real exceptions to the general pattern. Since a pattern exists, one may ask what effect was intended. Where the *waw*-consecutive stands first in the final line of a stanza, it seems reasonable to suppose that the verb was meant to mark and emphasize the end of the strophe. The effect of the second characteristic use is discussed in the NOTE at 3:2.

*Zion.* The literal translation of the Hebrew is "Daughter Zion."

7. Note that in the MT and the ancient versions there are four lines. After line 1 (7a) comes "All the precious things she had in olden times" (if this line, 7b, is included, the Hebrew of 7a would be translated in a slightly different way: "Jerusalem calls to mind, during the days when she was banished in misery," etc.). Since the rigid stanza-form rules out a four-line stanza in this chapter (as also in 2:19), most commentators have preferred to leave out the MT's 7b as interrupting the thought sequence, in preference to omitting 7c or 7d (7a must be kept for the acrostic), and I have done the same here. Recently Rudolph (1962) and Albrektson (1963), following Ehrlich (1914), have argued for eliminating the line beginning "When her people" (7c). They argue that to say "Jerusalem calls to mind the days," as one must if 7b is omitted, would mean that those days are in the past—which is not the case, as shown by the rest of the poem. Yet the "days" seems to be explained by 7c, "When her people fell into the enemy's grasp," as a reference to

the actual days of the fall of the city and the beginning of the Exile, a period that was in the past from the writer's point of view. Since acceptable sense is obtained, in fact, whether 7b or 7c is omitted, it is perhaps best to conclude with Meek (1956) that this strophe circulated in two different text-forms with identical first and third lines, the extant text being a conflation of the two. There seems little decisive reason to prefer either reading as the original.

Instead of eliminating the extra line from this stanza, and from 2:19, D. N. Freedman defends the longer text in both cases, demonstrating, in a series of careful discussions, that the inclusion of these (and other) irregular stanzas does not affect the correlation of the first three poems in Lamentations as far as length is concerned. "Length" is determined in this case by counting the syllables in each poem. Freedman asserts that the poet "was guided or limited by features governing overall length, and the need to achieve an effective balance between longer and shorter stanzas" (1972b: 374). The present writer is unconvinced that an ideal overall length was an aim of the author, and prefers to think that a uniform stanza pattern was characteristic of the original composition, and that this pattern has in a few places been obscured in the process of textual transmission.

4QLam[a] presents numerous variants throughout this verse (see "Collation of 4QLam[a] with MT," above, in the INTRODUCTION). In Cross's judgment, if the MT is corrupt in this verse, 4QLam[a] here gives "a badly corrupt text also." (Cross, 1983) In my judgment, it is not even a good starting point for correcting the MT. From the very beginning the text of this verse goes astray in 4QLam[a], which turns the first line of v 7, a statement about Jerusalem in the MT, into a direct appeal to Yahweh. This wording is suspect, for reasons given in the INTRODUCTION and because the direct address does not continue even through the subsequent text of the verse in 4QLam[a]!

*when she was banished in misery.* Heb m<sup>e</sup>rūdehā is rare and of uncertain meaning. It seems to form a hendiadys with ʿonyāh, to judge from similar juxtapositions at 3:19 and Isa 58:7 (if the text of these passages is in order), and is so translated here. The Greek renders m<sup>e</sup>rūdehā with apōsmos 'repulsion, driving away'.

*fell into the enemy's grasp.* In this context, where not only death but also exile is in the picture, this translation for Heb binpōl ʿammāh b<sup>e</sup>yad ṣār seems preferable to "Fell *by* the enemy's hand."

The latter translation is possible but is not the only acceptable rendering of the Hebrew phrase (contra Ehrlich 1914, followed by Meek 1956): note especially 2 Sam 24:14.

*collapse.* Heb *mišbattehā* is a *hapax legomenon*, often emended by commentators, but since it may well be related to *šābat* 'to stop, cease', and the sense thus obtained fits the context well, the MT is best retained. Here 4QLam[a] has *mšbryh* 'her ruins' (Cross). Perhaps this is also a case of banalization. In Albrektson's view (1963: ad loc.), Syr *tbara* probably does not indicate that the Hebrew text had a word derived from *šbr*; now that the reading of 4QLam[a] is available, one may perhaps regard this question as open; in any case the reading of the MT seems preferable.

8. *people shake their heads at her.* Literally, "For that reason she has become a *nīdāh*." Heb *nīdāh* occurs only here, and there are three main ways of explaining the reading and the sense. (1) Ibn Ezra, and in modern times Löhr and Rudolph, take it to mean "object of head-nodding," in other words, "object of scorn," comparing the *hiphʿil* form *hēnīd bᵉrōš* 'shake the head'; cf., for example, Jer 18:16; Ps 44:15 [ = 14E]. *nydh* would be of the same noun pattern as *bynh* from the root *byn*, or *qymh* (as in Lam 3:63) from *qwm*. The reading of the MT, explained in this way, has been followed here (so also Gordis 1967). (2) Note the variant of 4QLam[a] *lnwd* 'to wander'(?). Compare the LXX and the medieval Jewish commentator Rashi, who connects *nīdāh* with *nūd* 'to wander'. But we do not know of a noun *nwd* except for the single occurrence in a textually difficult passage, Ps 56:9, and it seems unacceptable to suppose that we have here what is apparently an infinitive form *nwd* used in the sense of an abstract noun, "a group of wanderers." Yet there is a rare noun *nyd* in Job 16:5: *nyd śpty*. (3) Either of the preceding explanations seems preferable to the third possibility, changing the text to *niddāh* 'unclean (i.e., menstruating) woman'. Even though this reading is reflected in Aquila, Symmachus, and the Syriac and is favored by many moderns, it seems to be a case of substitution of a well-known, hence easier, word, for a rare one.

*aloud.* Heb *gam* is ordinarily "also, too," but this sense is inappropriate here. A homonym *gm* 'aloud' (or the like) occurs often in Ugaritic with the verb *ṣh* 'to cry out' and has been identified with some plausibility in a number of biblical passages. McDaniel first suggested that *gam* means "aloud" in this passage (see 1968b: 31–32, with references to other notes on the subject).

9. The text of 9b seems rather short, since there are only two words, and accents, in the first colon. The use of *waw*-consecutive is also unusual compared to the general pattern in Lamentations (see the NOTE on v 6). One might suppose, then, that a verb has been lost at the beginning of the line, and that *wattēred* was originally the second verb in the kind of coordinate construction common in the book. It would be hazardous to restore the missing word, but it may have been something like "she has fallen."

10. The last line, especially the third, is an instance of the second colon in the line being longer than the first, if the Hebrew text is divided as the syntax seems to suggest.

11. For the MT's (qere) *mḥmdyhm*, (ketib) *mḥmwdyhm*, 4QLam[a] has *mḥmdyh*. The fem. sing. suffix "her" is reflected also in the LXX and Syriac, and in a Kennicott manuscript, according to Albrektson (1963), but the resulting sense is no improvement over the MT: what treasure did Zion have left to give? The variant of 4QLam[a] comes after a considerable haplography, which makes the case hard to decide. The suffix on 4QLam[a] *npšh* 'her soul/life' (MT *npš* 'life') is consistent with the previous fem. sing. suffix.

12. *Come, all you.* The MT's *lō 'ᵃlēkem*, literally, "no/not to you," is generally conceded to be corrupt in some way, though some have defended it. The reading of 4QLam[a] (for MT *'lykm kl* it has perhaps *'lyk[.]hkwl*) is "uncertain in part" (Cross 1983) and may only be an apparent variant. If *mem* did stand in the break, 4QLam[a] would be the practical equivalent of the MT here, with only a difference in spelling, but Cross believes there is no room for *mem*. Unfortunately, then, the new manuscript has no significant bearing on the old textual problem. Ancient Jewish tradition (see Caro 1893) took the *lō 'ᵃlēkem* as "may it not come upon you" and some moderns have explained the text so, but this is forced. Of various efforts to emend the text, the conjecture *lᵉkū* 'come', proposed by F. Praetorius (1895: 143), has the merit of being simple and of bearing some resemblance to the existing text, so it has been followed here as approximately correct. To the sequence "Come" followed by a question beginning with *'im*, one may compare Isa 1:18: "Come . . . if your sins are as scarlet," etc.

*which he caused me.* Heb *'ōlal* is a passive verb as pointed in the

MT, but since "Yahweh" is explicitly mentioned as the subject of an active verb in the next line, it seems preferable to suppose that this is one of the cases in which the text has been very slightly retouched to avoid ascribing to Yahweh the responsibility for pain or the like. See the NOTE on 4:16 below. "Yahweh" is the subject of *'ōlēl* in v 22.

*Which the* LORD *inflicted on me.* For MT *hwgh* 4QLam[a] has *hwgyrny*, which Cross (1983) prefers to the MT, translating the line "Wherewith Yahweh has terrified me," taking the verb as *hiph'il* of *ygr* (otherwise unattested; also the related *gwr* occurs only in *qal*). But the LXX support he cites is illusory; the LXX uses its regular equivalent for *hwgh*, and the suffix of the LXX and Syriac can readily be explained as supplied by the translators. With the 4QLam[a] reading, the Hebrew syntax seems odd ("wherewith" is forced).

*on the day of his anger?* For the MT's *ḥrwn 'pw* 4QLam[a] has *ḥrwnw*. This striking short reading, apparently the only biblical occurrence of "day of his anger" (*ywm ḥrwnw*), seems preferable to the longer and conventional MT.

13. *sank it.* Read *yōrīdennāh*, reversing the order of *w* and *y* at the beginning of MT *wayyirdennāh*. The LXX, which is very consistent otherwise in rendering Hebrew *waw*-consecutive by *kai*, does not have *kai* here and supports the proposed reading. The reading of the MT breaks the line at an unsatisfactory place, and the implied verb *rādāh* 'to rule' yields no satisfactory sense. Note that *yārad* 'to come down' is used of fire from God, as proposed here, in 2 Kgs 1:10, 12, 14; and 2 Chr 7:1. Use of an imperfect for past time, after a perfect in the first half line, is unusual, and not paralleled exactly anywhere else in Lamentations; but occasionally one does find a rather similar sequence of forms (cf. 1:14a; 2:22; 4:1–2), so this is perhaps not an insuperable objection to the emendation. For defense of the MT and a sense "which has subjected them" (my bones), see Barthélemy 1986.

*desolate, sick.* The speaker of these lines is obviously female, as throughout this section, but these adjectives seem to me too general and inexplicit to demonstrate that here we must think of menstrual distress, as suggested by Barbara Bakke Kaiser (citing 2 Sam 13:20), "Poet as 'Female Impersonator': The Image of Daughter

Zion as Speaker in Biblical Poems of Suffering," *Journal of Religion* 67 (1987): 164–82.

14. The text and sense of the first line have long puzzled commentators. For MT *nśqd*, of uncertain sense, 4QLam[a] has *nqśrh*, apparently a form of *qśr* 'to bind'; and for MT *yśtrqw*, of uncertain meaning, 4QLam[a] has *wyśtrq*, apparently the same word in a different grammatical form, which in turn implies a different syntactic division. I do not see in the reading of 4QLam[a] a starting point toward solution of the old *crux*. My translation of 14a, conjectural in many respects, is based on retaining the consonants of MT, but making some minor changes. (1) I read *niśqad* (with some Hebrew manuscripts) for *niśqad*. *niśqad* is a *hapax legomenon*, which may have arisen after other parts of the line had been misunderstood; *niśqad* would be the *niph'al* (not otherwise attested) of *śqd*, a well-known verb regularly followed by *'al*, which may easily read here, dropping the vowel-letter of *'ōl*. The verb is used in a hostile sense here, as in Jer 5:6; 44:27; Dan 9:14. (2) I read not *pešā'ay* 'my sins', which does not fit as subject of "are entangled," *yiśtār<sup>e</sup>gū*, in the following clause, but rather *pešā'ay* 'my steps', a rare word found in 1 Sam 20:3 and perhaps to be restored in Prov 29:6; a related verbal form occurs in Isa 27:4. (Perles 1922 already suggested *pešā'ay*, but treated the rest of the clause differently.) *śārag* is used only one other time in the Hebrew of the Bible, and hence biblical evidence alone is not likely to indicate adequately the range of meaning and usage of the verb. In Syr *srag* is used of a path: *'urḥā dabtuqlātā srīgā (h)wāt* 'a road beset *or* entangled with stumbling blocks', cited from R. Payne Smith, *Compendious Syriac Dictionary* (Oxford, 1903), s.v. *srag*. For the idea expressed, see the COMMENT below. This rendering may at least claim to respect the consonantal text, and is perhaps defensible linguistically; but it is, of course, far from certain. Praetorius proposed (1895: 143–44): "The yoke of my sins is heavy (*niqšāh 'ōl pešā'ay*)," and has been followed by others, including recently Kraus (1968). Already the Targum translated *niśqad* as "was heavy." Rudolph (1962) modifies Praetorius's suggestion: "My sins weigh heavy on me (*niqšū 'ālay pešā'ay*)."

*His yoke.* Read *'ullō*, with 4QLam[a] and Symmachus, for MT *'ālū* 'they have gone up'. The MT has perhaps been influenced by the plural ending of the preceding verb. But a plural verb does not agree with the singular verb later in the line, "He/it has brought low." Possibly, however, the original text has been partially lost through haplography, and we should read *'ālāh 'ullō 'al*, etc., "His yoke has gone up on," etc. Compare the NOTE on 5:5 below. Rudolph (1962), following Budde (1898), favors a similar solution.

The syntax of 14c is somewhat unusual, but the MT is retained here on the supposition that the clause following *bīdē* is a relative clause without relative pronoun, following a noun in construct (so Rudolph 1962 and others; see Barthélemy 1986).

*The* LORD. *'adōnāy* occurs fourteen times in Lamentations; *yhwh* 'Yahweh', the proper name of God, occurs thirty-two times. Aside from the isolated *'ēl* 'God' at 3:41 and *'elyōn* 'Most High' in 3:35, 38, these are the only divine names in the book. Rather strikingly, *'elōhīm* 'God' does not occur at all. The variation between *'adōnāy* and *yhwh* seems to be haphazard. There is no convincing explanation for it from the point of view of meaning, for in a given passage one seems about as appropriate as the other. Also metrically there is no apparent ground for preference of one over the other. Finally, one may note that there is considerable variation between the two in the manuscript tradition. It seems impossible to be sure that the usage was absolutely uniform even in the original form of the book, even though it is likely that to some extent *'adōnāy* had replaced an original *yhwh*, especially since in later periods *'adōnāy* was being pronounced in public reading wherever *yhwh* stood in the text. The practice in the present translation is to follow the reading given by Codex Petroburgensis, the manuscript printed in *BHS*, in the absence of any certain criterion for determining the original reading in a given verse.

15. *heaped up.* The verb *sillāh* with which the verse begins is difficult. It is often rendered "despised" or "flouted" (RSV), as if from a rare verb *slh* 'to despise' (elsewhere only at Ps 119:118 and there in *qal*, not *pi'el*), but this does not fit the subsequent "in my midst," which seems to demand a verb describing a physical action. The translation "heaped up" is based on seeing here a root *slh* (*sly*) equal in sense to the well-attested *sll* 'to heap up'. (Alternately, one might suppose that *sillāh* is a scribal error for a form of *sll*.) *sll* is used in Jer 50:26 of heaping up sheaves of grain ("sheaves" is a widely accepted correction, involving metathesis of two consonants, for an otherwise unintelligible word) preparatory to threshing; this is in turn a picture of the punishment to be inflicted on Babylon.

Note that the Targum here has *kᵉnas* 'gathered'. If it is correct to translate "heap up" here, the imagery of the verse is consistent, harvest metaphors being used throughout (see the COMMENT below). The Syriac renders *sillāh* by *kbaš* 'he trampled down'; which etymology the translator had in mind is not clear.

16. In 4QLamᵃ the *pe* stanza (v 17) comes before the *ayin* stanza, as is the case also in chaps. 2, 3, and 4 in the MT (for a discussion, see the INTRODUCTION). In the case of chap. 1, there seems to be little firm basis for choosing between the order of the MT (followed here) and that of 4QLamᵃ.

*my eyes*. For the first line of the verse, 4QLamᵃ has a text shorter than the MT and different in details. Welcome confirmation of an old conjecture comes where the MT has ʿēnî ʿēnî 'my eye, my eye', a clear case of dittography (i.e., of copying one word twice by mistake). Read simply ʿēnî, with 4QLamᵃ, LXX, Syriac, and Vg. Note that a more normal meter, with the second colon shorter than the first, is obtained by deleting one ʿenî as a dittography. (The Targum cleverly renders the MT by "my two eyes"!)

Beyond this detail, the value of the variants of 4QLamᵃ is questionable. Cross's reconstructed short text, "My eye weeps" (1983), is not very close to either the MT or 4QLamᵃ, and encounters the objection that in Biblical Hebrew usage the subject of the verb "to weep" is never the eye, always a person. The difficult reading of 4QLamᵃ, ʿl ʾlh bkw ʿyny yrdh dmʿty, might be thought to have arisen from *ʿl ʾlh bkw <ʾbkh> ʿyny yrdh dmʿty 'Over these things I weep copiously; my eye runs with my tears', whose merits could be weighed against the MT wording.

*desolate*. Heb *šōmēmîm* is an adjective usually used of cities, less often of people, as here (so 2 Sam 13:20; Isa 54:1).

17. The *b* in *bᵉyādehā* is instrumental (lit., "with her hands"); cf. Josh 8:18.

*commanded*. For MT *ṣwh* 4QLamᵃ has *ṣph*, which Cross (1983) renders "kept watch." But the MT's version seems to be acceptable Hebrew usage; a literal rendering would be "Yahweh gave command concerning Jacob," with the following clause supplying the content of the command: "his enemies (should be) around him. In Isa 23:11 the sequence is "Yahweh gave command concerning Canaan" with an infinitive phrase following, which supplies the content of the command: "to destroy his strongholds"; cf. Isa 10:6; Jer 47:7; Ps 91:11, "he shall give his angels charge over thee." Cross's rendering of the whole line is strained, which points to the difficulty in adopting the reading of 4QLam[a].

*unclean.* In other words, menstruous, hence ceremonially impure. Parallels to this metaphoric use are found in Isa 30:22; 64:5 [ = 6E]; Ezek 7:19–20; Ezra 9:11. For MT *lndh bynyhm*, 4QLam[a] has *lndwh bnyhmh* ('to reject their sons'?); it seems best to regard this wording as a corruption (perhaps arising from graphic confusion; so Cross 1983).

18. The appeal to "all peoples" to hear is relatively rare; a fairly close parallel is Ps 49:1 [ = 2E]; cf. 1 Kgs 22:28; Mic 1:2.

19. *they deceived me.* McDaniel has argued (1968b: 33–34) that *hēmmāh* here should be taken as the Hebrew counterpart of Ug *hm* 'behold', and it must be conceded that "they" is slightly out of place in this line, where no emphasis on the pronominal subject is clearly intended. But v 8 *(hī')* and possibly v 21 *('attāh)* seem to provide parallel examples of an independent pronoun being used as verbal subject for no obvious reason as far as sense is concerned. In that case, one suspects that metrical considerations have dictated the use of the pronoun, an explanation that would cover the present case also.

On the meaning of "lovers" cf. the COMMENT on v 2.

The rest of this verse is somewhat difficult, hence the text translated here is possibly not correct. The second line is short, being 2 + 2 according to the principle of counting accents, and therefore some suggest that a word has been lost. Note, however, that there are other relatively short lines in this chapter (2b, 4c, 8c, 13c), so that this line is perhaps not impossible as it stands. In structure it is very similar to 18c, as pointed out to me by D. N. Freedman. In the third line, the LXX and Syriac add, "and they did not find (any)." Some commentators (recently Kraus 1968) have accepted this wording as the original second half of the line and delete the MT's "to keep alive," which is syntactically somewhat difficult. But it seems more likely that "and they did not find (any)" is an explanatory addition to the difficult MT (so Albrektson 1963). The MT is kept here, then, especially since the syntax—perfect verb followed by imperfect verb with the conjunction *waw*, expressing purpose—

is not totally unparalleled; see BDB, s.v. *w*, where 2 Kgs 19:25 and Isa 25:9 are cited as comparisons.

20. *My heart is turned over.* . . . Cf. Hos 11:8. NJV translates "I know how wrong I was to disobey," comparing Exod 14:5.

*I was very rebellious.* If the *kî* is taken as asseverative, a translation "How rebellious I was!" would also be possible. C. L. Seow, "A Textual Note on Lamentations 1:20," *CBQ* 47 (1985): 416–19 understands the conjunction thus and goes on to propose a slight emendation (reading forms of *mrr* 'to be bitter' instead of *mrh* 'to rebel'), yielding "how bitter am I." The versional evidence cited is perhaps too inconclusive to demonstrate the superiority of this reading to the MT's.

*famine.* Read *kāpān* (cf. Job 5:22; 30:3 and Aram *kapnā'*) for MT *kammāwet* 'like death', which it seems to me cannot be made to yield satisfactory sense despite repeated efforts by interpreters to defend it. Or perhaps read *\*kapnūt*, cf. Syr *kapnūtā*; though unattested in Hebrew, the form with abstract termination would better explain the development of the MT. The present conjecture is based especially on Ezek 7:15: "The sword outside, and pestilence and famine inside; he who is in the field shall die by the sword, and he who is in the city—famine and pestilence shall devour him"; and Jer 14:18: "If I go out to the field, there are those slain by the sword, and if I go into the city, there are the diseases of famine." Cf. also Deut 32:25: "In the open the sword shall bereave, and in the chambers shall be terror" (*RSV*), and from the "Lamentation over the Destruction of Sumer and Ur," *ANET*, p. 618, lines 403–4: "Ur . . . inside it we die of famine / Outside we are killed by the weapons of Elamites."

21. *Listen.* Based on repointing as imperative instead of the perfect ("they heard") of MT, which may have arisen under the influence of the perfect *sāmᵉ'ū* of the next line. In view of the other singular imperatives or precatives addressed to God in the immediate context, a singular imperative, which would imply that Yahweh is addressed (so the Syriac), is preferable to a plural, which would be addressed to other men or peoples (so the Greek; cf. v 18).

The second line of this verse (21b) is much the longest line in the chapter. Commentators have favored dropping various words or phrases. Possibly the line is a conflation of two variants:

1. All my enemies—*heard of my trouble*—that you had done it.

2. All my enemies—*rejoiced*—that you had done it.

*Oh bring on . . . !* Many have rendered this verb as imperative, which the context favors, by emending the MT *hēbē'tā* to imperative *hābē'*; commonly the Syriac version is cited in favor of the change. Although the result is the same, note that the present translation is based on taking *hēbē'tā* as a case wherein the perfect is used to express a wish or request, a use that seems to be attested elsewhere in the book; cf. 4:22 and especially 3:55–66 passim, where perfects alternate with imperatives and other expressions of volitive ideas. Scholars disagree on the question of whether the perfect is used in this way in Hebrew, and on how commonly it may have been used. But it seems best to recognize that the author of Lamentations occasionally uses the perfect to express wishes and requests, rather than to emend away all such occurrences or resort to other explanations. For other discussions of this construction in Hebrew, see Bergsträsser, *Hebräische Grammatik*, 2d ed., para. 6i; Carl Brockelmann, *Grundriss* II (Berlin, 1908), 29–30; Paul Joüon, *Grammaire de l'hébreu biblique*, 2d ed. (Rome, 1947), para. 112k; Mitchell Dahood, "Ugaritic-Hebrew Syntax and Style," *Ugarit-Forschungen* 1 (Neukirchen-Vluyn, 1969), 20 n. 7, and his "Grammar of the Psalter," in *Psalms III, 101–150*, AB 17C (Garden City, N.Y., 1970), pp. 414–17.

# COMMENT

The first of the five Lamentations is an exceptionally impressive poetic depiction of the desolation of the city of God. From one point of view, the poem is a series of brief pictures of the distress, none sustained for very long, and mostly traditional, derived from images and ideas common in Israelite poetic laments. This form creates a certain evenness of mood, a notable contribution to this effect being the fivefold repetition of the theme "there is no one to comfort her" (1:2, 9, 16, 17, 21). Thus superficially viewed, the form of the poem is contributed by an external device, the alphabetic acrostic (see the INTRODUCTION), there being no easily observable outline or logical progression of thought or action. Such a view, however, misses the poet's intent. His aim, we may infer, was not to write a poem moving to an obvious climax of action or thought, but rather to create one of essentially uniform tone, corresponding to the one appalling catastrophe and the unvarying misery that came with it and followed it. A man who has just lost a wife or child cannot keep his mind off it, and that is how this poet writes, ever returning to the source of his grief.

Yet there is a definite psychological progress in the poem; it moves from an external, objective, third-person view to an internal, subjective, first-person view. This shift contributes the movement and organization that are lacking at other levels of the poem. Two persons speak. The first is the poet himself. He writes of Zion in the third person, as one observing from outside what has happened to her, and the reasons for it. This is the point of view through almost exactly half of the poem, vv 1–11. It is broken, however, by the brief ejaculatory prayer at 9c and 11c: "LORD, look upon my misery!" and "O LORD, look and consider how worthless I have become!" These exclamations prepare the way for the shift in speaker from v 12 on (one could also argue that part two begins at 11c). From this point on it is Zion herself who speaks, and the more detached voice is only occasionally heard (15c, 17). This midway division is indicated in the chapter outline, below.

A.  The anguish of Zion, seen from without, vv 1–11 (with brief prayers by Zion herself, 9c and 11c)

B.  Zion's anguish, as she herself feels it, vv 12–22 (with recurrence of the previous point of view in 15c, 17)

This shift to the point of the personified Zion achieves several things. One effect is to heighten the expression of anguish, and to intensify the participation in this anguish by the worshiper when the poem is used liturgically. At the same time, the introduction at this point of Zion herself as the speaker is a means by which the poet expresses the central tragedy in the situation. The point of the book is not just that a nation has fallen and that a man (or the group of survivors as a whole) is grieved, but that a greater thing, a greater person, is in anguish: Zion, the city of God, the community of the elect, who in her historical being is not identical with those alive at any one time. Appropriately, then, the first "I" in the book is not the "I" of an individual, even as the spokesman for the survivors, but of Zion herself. Thus through this personification the poet is able to use very personal, emotional language, but at the same time to transcend the merely subjective. Finally, one may observe that the use of first-person speech by Zion here affects our reaction to the use of first-person forms elsewhere: the use of "I" by the poet himself, or of "we" by the surviving community, and so on. We are prepared by chapter 1 for the appearance of an individual as representative of the people, and for the idea that one person's suffering can depict, or help explain, or even relieve, the suffering of the city of God—a point that becomes especially important for chapter 3.

It seems likely that the first poem was intended from the outset for use in congregational worship, like the other poems in the book (see the INTRODUCTION). Nevertheless, the idea that it received a kind of dramatic performance, with different persons speaking the parts of Zion, of the poet, and so on—a hypothesis that has been advanced by Wiesmann 1954 and H.-J. Kraus 1968 (Kraus does not press the hypothesis) among others—seems speculative in the extreme.

On the date of chapter 1, which is taken here to be the same as that of the other chapters, see the INTRODUCTION. There too the reader will find a brief discussion of the literary genre or genres to which this poem belongs, and a defense of the viewpoint adopted in the present commentary, which is that identification of this poem as a funeral song or the like tends to hinder rather than advance understanding of it.

"How" (Heb *'ēkāh*; elsewhere also *'ēk*) is a traditional way of beginning a poem that depicts a striking change: from virtue to vice, for example, in Isa 1:21; or, often, from a glorious past to a miserable present. The latter use accounts for its frequent occurrence in laments and funeral songs (cf. 2:1; 4:1; Jer 48:17; Isa 14:4; Jer 9:18 [ = 19E]; Ezek 26:17). The effect is to make of what follows an incredulous question: "How can it be that . . . ?"—an expression of the speaker's astonishment, grief, or indignation at what has happened.

The opening stanza (v 1) is one of the most carefully worked out in the book from a formal point of view. The three lines are parallel to each other (so-called "external parallelism"). The first two are linked by repetition of *rabbātī* (a repetition not reproduced in the present translation), and the third is closely joined to them by the parallel word *śārātī*. This is, however, placed in a chiastic position, that is, it is in the opposite position in the line with respect to its counterpart, *rabbātī*. This formal elaborateness marks the importance of the themes introduced. At once we encounter the picture of Zion as a person, a mourning woman. As stated above, this image becomes of increasing importance throughout the poem, and in other parts of the book as well. Simultaneously another theme appears, the contrast of former glories to present desolation and humiliation. This is a common element in laments and funeral songs ("How the mighty have fallen!"), but here there is a significant addition. It lies in the element of hyperbole involved in calling Jerusalem "greatest among nations" and "noblest of states." Aside from its rhetorical effect, as heightening the contrast, these words recall the extravagant, semimythical language used of Zion in, for example, Ps 48:2–3 [ = 1–2E]: "His holy mountain, beautiful in elevation, the joy of all the earth, Mount Zion, on the slopes of Zaphon." This language belongs to a description of Jerusalem, not as she ever was in fact, but as she was in the eyes of those who believed her to be the city of God. We have here, then, a less explicit anticipation of the question of 2:15: "Is this the city they call the perfection of beauty" (or ". . . the joy of all the earth?"; see the NOTE ad loc.). Jerusalem is compared to a widow because widows, together with orphans, were the most defenseless people in ancient society (cf. 5:3; Isa 49:20–21; 51:18; 54:4–6), and the most to be pitied.

The next stanza (v 2) continues the personification but adds a new theme—Zion as the faithless woman. Thereby another major concern of the book is given early announcement: Why did it happen? By using an ambiguous image the poet manages to stress two different elements: the pathos of the situation and the nature of Zion's guilt. When it is said "All her friends have betrayed her," this is what is commonly said in laments: that the sufferer's friends have forsaken him and become hostile (Ps 88:19 [ = 18E]; 38:12 [ = 11E]; cf. also the Babylonian "Poem of the Righteous Sufferer" [*Ludlul bēl nēmeqi*], tablet I, lines 84–88: "My friend has become foe," etc., in W. G. Lambert, *Babylonian Wisdom Literature* [Oxford, 1960], p. 35). The lovers and friends in the present case may be figurative, however, for the faithless allies of Israel. In the metaphorical language familiar especially from Hosea, Jeremiah, and Ezekiel, Israel, the wife of Yahweh, has been unfaithful to him by entering into alliance with other nations and gods (e.g., Hos 8:9–10; Ezek 16:28–29; 23:5–21). These paramours in the end forsake her (Hos 2:9 [ = 7E]; Jer 22:20–22; 30:14) or turn against her (Ezek 16:37–41; 23:22–29; cf. also v 19 below). Because only Yahweh was supposed to be Israel's overlord, and the one who protected her and fought her battles, the prophets regarded it as the most serious kind of apostasy when Israel put herself under the rule of some earthly kingdom. This point of view is shared by the writer of Lamentations: compare 5:6–7.

If the Hebrew of v 3 is correctly translated here (see the NOTE), the whole verse refers to Judah's troubles in the time before the final collapse. Even though she "dwelled among the nations," that is, existed as an independent nation, she did not in her latter days enjoy "rest." The last word is of considerable weight: "rest" in the Promised Land was an important part of Israel's conception of what belonged to her as God's people, and its removal was a sign that his favor had departed. On "rest" compare 5:5 and Gerhard von Rad, "There Remains Still a Rest for the People of God: An Investigation of a Biblical Conception," in *The Problem of the Hexateuch and Other Essays* (Edinburgh and London, 1966), 94–102.

The elements mentioned in v 4 combine reasonably well to depict desolate Jerusalem as deprived of religious festivals. The highways mourn, lacking any pilgrims; and gates, the focus of festive coming and going, are deserted. The priests, once vitally active at the great feasts, now sigh. To account for mention of the "young women" or "virgins" (Heb $b^e t\bar{u}l\bar{o}t$), commentators have pointed, with some plausibility, to mention of virgins or young women as having a role in festal celebrations, for example, Jer 31:13 and Judg 21:19–21. With "and she is bitter," the personified Zion is again the subject. One may go farther, however, and suggest that the poet's picture has been shaped, whether he was conscious of it or not, by the city-lament tradition (see above, in the INTRODUCTION), with its central female figure, blended with traditional descriptions of ritual mourning, specifically in time of drought. The theme "the land mourns in drought" appears in longer and shorter forms at numerous points in biblical literature. Typical elements include, first, the statement that the land "mourns" or "is dried up" (Heb 'ābal; cf. Joel 1:10; Jer 14:2; Hos 4:3). The alternative translations are given because 'ābal means both; lexicographers disagree about whether one root or two is involved, see KB[3] s.v.; Joseph Scharbert, *Der Schmerz im Alten Testament*, Bonner Biblische Beiträge 8 (Bonn, 1955), 47–58; also Lohfink 1962: 274–75. The question need not concern us here, for there can be no doubt that speakers of Hebrew associated the two, even if only as homonyms, so that even in a context wherein the meaning "to dry up" is appropriate, associations with "mourning" are present. In examples of the topos under consideration, not only the earth is said to mourn (dry up), but also "gates," as in the present passage; compare Jer 14:2; Isa 3:26; Lam 2:8. In this sort of description, there is commonly found a listing of what has been taken away; for example, birds, beasts, and even fish, Hos 4:3; cattle and birds, Jer 12:4; vintagers and more, Isa 16:10. This element is perhaps present in the words "none come in for the feasts" of the present verse. When nature mourns, people also mourn; either the same verb 'ābal is used (Joel 1:9) or the closely associated term 'umlal (Hos 4:3; cf. Isa 19:8); or the mourning activity is otherwise described: Jer 14:2; Isa 3:26; 19:8. The priests, mentioned as sighing in the passage under discussion, appear prominently in Joel 1:9, 13, where they are urged to mourn and weep. In the same passage (Joel 1:8) one discovers in a simile, a parallel to the "virgins" here in v 4: "Lament like a virgin girded with sackcloth for the husband of her youth." Jer 31:12–14 depicts a glorious time when "I will turn their mourning into joy," and is a kind of mirror image of the mourning topos: grain, wine, and oil and the young of flocks and herds are promised along with plentiful water, the young women will rejoice in the dance, and the priests will have great abundance to eat. It is obvious that a very similar assembly of elements has gone into making up the description. If one pushes still farther back, one may propose that the elements brought together in this literary theme were originally associated with the mourning for the dead god of fertility. The mourning for such a figure is referred to in Ezek 8:14 and Zech 12:10–14, and is depicted with considerable fullness in the Baal epic, for which see *ANET*, p. 138 (I\* AB vi 9–22 = *CTA* 5; *UT* 67), where the Virgin *(btlt)* Anat is the principal mourner, *ANET*, pp. 139–40 (I AB i 1–18 = *CTA* 6; *UT* 49 + 62). (On echoes of the Canaanite myth in the Old Testament, with specific reference to Joel 1:8, see H. W. Wolff on Joel [in *Biblischer Kommentar*], with references to studies by F. F. Hvidberg, A. S. Kapelrud, and Miloš Bič.) For a fuller discussion, see my article in *Perspective* 12 (1971): 121–33.

The writer of Lamentations was very strongly under the influence of inherited literary patterns, in both obvious and subtle ways. He has cast his observations into inherited, age-old forms—in fact, at these points it would be correct to say that the traditional literary forms shaped his perceptions and memories of the events.

"Her enemies are now supreme" (v 5) would be, in a more literal rendering, "Her enemies have become the head," an allusion to "He [the alien in Israel's midst] will become the head, and you will become the tail" (Deut 28:44, cf. 28:13). An ancient midrash on Lamentations already connects the two: "Had you been worthy, you would have read in the Torah, 'And the Lord will make thee the head,' but now that you are unworthy, you read, 'Her adversaries are become the head' " (translation of A. Cohen, *Midrash Rabbah*, ed. H. Freedman and Maurice Simon, vol. 8 [London, 1939], 16). Thus this line indicates that the writer may have seen in the fate of Jerusalem the fulfillment of a threat, or curse, associated with the covenant with God. This same insight finds indirect expression elsewhere in the book: cf. 4:3–4, 10; 5:18, and possibly also 1:8; 2:16; 3:10–11; 4:6; 5:14–15. Deuteronomy 28 and Leviticus 26, both of which come at the end of lists of obligations imposed by the covenant with God, are the clearest biblical examples of the association of curses with covenant. On covenant forms in the ancient Near East and the Old Testament, see George Mendenhall, *Law and Covenant in Israel and in the Ancient Near East* (Pittsburgh, 1955); the role of the curses is treated on p. 34 there, and more fully in D. R. Hillers, *Treaty-Curses and the Old Testament Prophets* (Rome, 1964).

The second line (v 5b) continues and makes more explicit the political image implied in the first. Zion's sin is "rebellion *(pešaʿ)*," a term that is originally derived from political life, where it is a common term for revolt against an overlord (2 Kgs 1:1; 3:5; etc.).

The personification of Zion is brought to the fore again in the reference to the inhabitants of Judah as "her children."

The following stanza (v 6), loosely joined to the preceding by "and" (*waw*-consecutive, see the NOTE) is not closely linked with the foregoing in thought, but perhaps the idea of the children going away into exile suggested to the writer the departure of the glory of Israel with which the new stanza begins. After the general statement of line 1 follows a specific detail: the princes have been driven to the point of collapse, the idea being that this happened during the siege and flight from Jerusalem, or perhaps on the long road into captivity. The fate of the princes is cast in the form of a simile involving either "stags" (MT: *'ayyālīm*) or "rams" (*'ēlīm*, implied by LXX and Vg); the same consonantal text permits either interpretation. It is preferable to take this word as "stags," since the third line seems to be a continuation of the simile, and the hunting image fits better with stags than with rams. (For *rādap* in the sense "to hunt," cf. 1 Sam 26:20.) The enemy is compared to a hunter also in 3:52 and Jer 16:16. J. Rimbach has called my attention to a parallel in one of the curses of Esarhaddon's vassal treaties (lines 576–78): "Just as a stag is chased and killed, so may your avengers chase and kill you, your brothers, your sons" (translation of E. Reiner, *ANET*, p. 540). The simile is effective not only within this stanza but as a link to the last line of the preceding verse, since "before the hunter" echoes "before the enemy."

Part of Jerusalem's suffering was that, in her utter helplessness, her enemies laughed when they saw her (v 7). This is a common motif in a variety of Old Testament contexts. It is used of an individual in Lam 3:14 and Pss 37:13; 52:8 [ = 6E]; Prov 1:26; Job 30:1. From use of individuals it is transferred to nations, and it occurs in laments for the community in Ps 44:15 [ = 14E]; 79:4; 80:7 [ = 6E]; cf. Jer 48:26, 39.

If v 8 is correctly translated here (see the NOTE), the picture of v 7 is carried on: Zion in her misery is the butt of scorn, expressed by derisive shaking of the head. There is a certain intensification in that here it is not just the enemy who laughs, but all who once respected her. Even if it is correct to keep the reading *nīdāh* ("object of scorn," lit., "nodding"; see the NOTE) the writer may have intended a pun on a word of similar sound, *niddāh* 'menstruous woman, unclean thing', for he introduces as the reason for the scorn that her revilers "saw her naked" (cf. Gordis, ad loc.). The same two ideas, exposure of nakedness (*'erwāh*) and uncleanness (*niddāh*), are associated in Lev 20:21 (cf. Ezek 22:10), hence it seems unlikely that the sequence here is entirely fortuitous. The motif "they saw her naked" is meaningful at several levels. It is primarily an expression of the utter contempt with which Zion is treated. Exposure of one's body, especially the genitals, was to the ancient Israelites an almost immeasurable disgrace, a shame they felt much more deeply than most moderns would. This attitude finds expression in the story of Noah's drunkenness (Gen 9:20–27) and in several idioms: "uncover the nakedness of so-and-so" is an expression for "enter into incestuous marriage" (Lev 18:6–18; 20:11–21), and "something exposed" is an idiom for something indecent in Deut 23:15 [ = 14E]; 24:1. Stripping was apparently part of the cruel treatment that might be meted out to a woman guilty of sexual misconduct (Ezek 16:35–39; 23:29; cf. Isa 3:17), and it is used metaphorically of the punishment of nations (Isa 47:2–3; Lam 4:21; Nah 3:5). This is the most obvious meaning of the line, but in addition one may note that being stripped bare is also a curse connected with treaties or covenants (see the COM-MENT on v 5, above). Finally, one may note that the expression "to see the nakedness" of a country is used (Gen 42:9, 12) of spying out its weakness from a strategic point of view, and it is possible that a play on this sense of the term is also involved here.

"Pollution," ritual uncleanness, is a not very euphemistic reference to menstrual blood (cf. Isa 64:5 [ = 6E]), but the exact point of the image—assuming that the writer had something very specific in mind—is difficult to determine. One finds elsewhere the idea that the innocent blood shed in a city makes it unclean (Ps 106:38–39 and cf. the COMMENT on 4:13–15); perhaps that is the idea here, but nothing in the immediate context prepares for it. Elsewhere one finds the notion that "whoredom" with idols or other nations makes the land (pictured as a woman) unclean, ritually impure; thus Hos 5:3; 6:10; Jer 2:23; Ezek 23:7, 13.

"She did not think of her future" (9a) seems to have no very close connection to the first half of the line. The identical words are used of Babylon, also in a poem in which she is personified as a humiliated woman, Isa 47:7. The point there is that she had always thought she would be a queen and did not give a moment's thought to the consequences of her actions. Hence this half line seems to be tied more closely to the second line of the stanza, with its reference to the fall of Jerusalem, than to the foregoing. The verb *yārad* 'to come down' is used of the humiliation of persons in Ezek 30:6 and Isa 47:1, and the same sense is evidently intended here also, the personification being continued. Note, however, that the verb is also used of the fall of a besieged city in Deut 20:20. Heb *pᵉlā'îm* (translated "astonishingly" here) does not occur elsewhere in this form or this kind of usage, and the exact nuance escapes us. Perhaps the idea is similar to that of 4:12: in view of Yahweh's promises, no one could believe that the enemy would take Jerusalem. Here, however, it is Jerusalem herself who did not believe that retribution awaited her. The verses close with a prayer that, as stated above, is to be thought of as spoken by the city herself, an anticipation of the shift in point of view that is carried out completely in v 12.

The heathen have reached out greedily for Zion's "precious things," which refers in this context to the temple treasures, which the Babylonians took away, 2 Kgs 25:13–17. The command referred to in the following lines is obviously Deut 23:4 [ = 3E], in view of the close verbal agreement: "No Ammonite or Moabite shall enter the assembly of Yahweh; not even the tenth generation of them shall enter the assembly of Yahweh, ever." Since the Babylonians (Chaldeans) were the ones who entered the temple, and since there is no evidence that Moabites and Ammonites figured in the destruction of Jerusalem at this time, it is evident that the Deuteronomic command has been broadened, if only by poetic license, to cover the "heathen," *gōyîm*, in general. (Later, in the time of Ezra and Nehemiah, the command was applied to all non-Israelites, and was taken as prohibiting intermarriage; see Neh 13:1–3.) Here in Lamentations, the reference to the commandment is made with ironic intention: no heathen was to enter, even piously and peaceably, into the sacred assembly, but now they break in violently and rob the holy place.

The final verse of this first half of the poem (11) reaches a climax of pathos. In order to get food, the survivors of the siege have sold their "darlings," that is, children, as explained already by Theodoret (died ca. A.D. 460). Heb *maḥᵃmaddēhem* (*qere*; *ketib* is probably meant to be *maḥᵃmūdēhem*) means "precious things" and may be used of possessions or treasures, as in v 10, but is used also of "precious children, darlings," for example, in Hos 9:16: "Even though they give birth, I will slay the darling offspring of their wombs *(maḥᵃmaddē biṭnām)*." Compare the expression *maḥᵃmaddē 'ayin,* which may refer to things, as in 1 Kgs 20:6; or to people, as in Ezek 24:16 and Lam 2:4. The picture of the Israelites giving up mere possessions to stay alive lacks poignancy. That they sell children to buy food is both more striking and better paralleled in ancient descriptions of famine, on which see especially A. L. Oppenheim, " 'Siege-Documents' from Nippur," *Iraq* 17 (1955): 69–89. Compare also the *Atra-hasīs* epic, where in a description of a great famine there occur the lines "When the fifth year arrived . . . the daughter watched the scales (at the sale) of the mother. The mother watched the scales (at the sale) of the daughter"; translation of W. G. Lambert and A. R. Millard, *Atra-hasīs* (Oxford, 1969), 113, the lines quoted being their manuscript S, Rev. vi, lines 9–10. This sale of members of the family is a stage preceding the final horror, cannibalism, mentioned both in Lamentations (4:10) and in *Atra-hasīs,* where it occurs in the year following the sales: "When the sixth year arrived they served up [the daughter] for dinner, They served up the son for food."

Like v 9, so also 11 closes with a brief prayer, spoken by Jerusalem. It seems likely that the poet meant to begin a new section precisely at the middle of his poem (v 12); otherwise one could also regard this prayer in 11c as beginning the second part of the poem.

Zion herself speaks now, and throughout almost all the rest of the poem. This climactic half of the chapter begins with a stanza that is appropriately general in its terms: all are urged to look and consider: "Is there any pain like my pain?" The detailed exposition of what the pain consists in, of what specifically Yahweh has done to her, is to be set forth in following verses. This reference to those who pass by is an exceedingly common motif in Old Testament literature. Usually it is as in Lam 2:15 (see the COMMENT there): those who pass by will mock, and the like. Here the sense is somewhat different, the best biblical parallel being Job 21:29, where Job, in response to the notion that the wicked suffer, asserts the contrary: "Haven't you asked those who pass on the road?" The passersby are a figurative representation of common human experience, the additional implication being that they are unbiased because uninvolved in what they see.

The intensification of feeling that is characteristic of the second half of the poem is noticeable already here in v 12. In part one, it is plainly stated only once (5b) that Yahweh is the one who has afflicted Zion, but from v 12 on this sort of statement is much more frequent. Yahweh has brought to pass "the day of his anger." The idea of a *dies irae*, a day of wrath belonging to Yahweh, is very widely attested in the Old Testament, beginning as early as Amos, nearly two hundred years before the present passage was written. Scholars disagree about exactly what the Israelite conception—or conceptions—of the day of Yahweh was at various times. The book of Lamentations is notable in that it several times (here and 2:1, 21, 22) refers to the day of Yahweh's wrath as past. The awful events of the siege and fall were already a decisive outpouring of Yahweh's wrath, a judgment day. (The author still looks for a future "day" of vengeance on the enemy, however; see v 21.)

The reference to "fire" in the first line of 13 would constitute a link to v 12, with its *"burning* anger," if the reading of the MT is retained. The picture of pain as fire shut up in one's bones occurs in a famous passage in Jeremiah (20:9). This and the following verse describe Zion's plight entirely in terms of the suffering of an individual, with language drawn from the repertory of biblical laments. Only in v 15 is there again reference to an actual event in the siege of Jerusalem. Actually, this consistent mode of presentation begins at v 12, where only the phrase "day of his anger" is a reference to the event.

Zion's trouble is like a net or trap, which was spread out in her path and which has ensnared her. This is an exceptionally common image in the Old Testament. God himself is said to spread a net for men here and in Jer 50:24; Ezek 12:13; 17:20; 32:3; Hos 7:12; cf. also Ps 94:13. "He turned me back" follows naturally on the image of the net in that it also is based on the comparison of a man's way of life to walking along a path—the divine punishment takes the form of obstacles to a man's walking; cf. Isa 28:13 for a similar association of ideas. "Desolate" and "sick" emphasize the subjective aspect of the suffering rather than the objective destruction, since closely parallel passages—Isa 1:5; Jer 8:18; Lam 1:22 and 5:17 —specifically refer to the "heart" as sick.

God has kept watch over his people's steps (see the NOTE for this translation, v 14), not to guard them but to trip them up. The idea is similar to that of 3:9: "he has made my paths crooked," and 3:10–11, where Yahweh is said to lie in wait like a bear or lion.

Next the poet presents the destruction of Jerusalem, especially of the people, as a grim harvest. (If the difficult first word of v 15 is correctly translated as "heap up"—see the NOTE—the whole verse maintains this theme.) Like sheaves stacked in the middle of the threshing floor, so the mighty men of Zion were gathered up in her midst. Then Yahweh called her enemies together to crush them. Similar harvest imagery is used of destruction or punishment in Jer 9:21 [ = 22E]; 51:33; Amos 1:3; Mic 4:12–13 ("For he has gathered them like sheaves to the threshing floor. Arise and thresh!"); Isa 41:15–16. Note that in Joel 4:13 [ = 3:13E] the picture of the grain harvest is followed by the image of the vintage, as here; the sequence was probably influenced by the order in the agricultural year. The lengthy, vivid expansion of this image of the "grapes of wrath" in Isa 63:1–6 makes explicit what is to be understood in the laconic statement of Lamentations. This first-person section of the chapter closes with the picture of mother Zion weeping, and the familiar theme recurs; "any comforter . . . is far from me" (v 16).

At v 17 there is a shift in emphasis, signaled by the momentary abandonment of the first person in favor of the third person, that is, the poet speaks about Zion, instead of Zion speaking for herself. Although Zion soon reappears, the rest of the poem is made different from what went before by two themes that may be said to dominate, even though the content of 17–22 is extremely varied and though there are agitated shifts from description of troubles, to complaint, to appeals for sympathy (for comments on individual verses, see also the NOTES). One new theme is a progressive turning toward Yahweh. In v 17 it is established that he is the author of the calamity, and in v 18 comes a confession that he is justified in what he has done. "The LORD is in the right" is an expression ultimately derived from legal language; it is the formula for pronouncing a verdict. Unexpressed here, but implied, is the other half of the formula, "and I am in the wrong." The following "for I disobeyed his command" supplies the basis for the verdict. Compare Exod 9:27; 1 Sam 24:18 [ = 17E]; 2 Kgs 10:9; Ps 119:137; Ezra 9:15. In religious language it is a formula for expressing humble submission to divine judgment; cf. especially Neh 9:33: "You are in the right with respect to all that has come upon us, for you have kept your word whereas we have behaved wrongly." Continuing this turning toward Yahweh, the last three verses are dominated by appeals to him to see (20), to hear (21), and finally (21–22) to bring retribution on the enemy (see the NOTE on the translation of 21c as a prayer). This retribution is to take the form of a "day" of judgment on the enemies. The assumption made is that Yahweh's sway is universal, and what he has already brought on Israel, "the day of his anger" (v 12), should also come on those who laughed at her fall. Compare 3:58–66 and 4:21–22.

The second dominant characteristic of this final portion of the poem is the recurrence of statements made earlier. "See my pain" (18) echoes 12a and b; "My young men and women have been taken prisoner" (18) is a modification of 5c; "I called for my lovers" (19) recalls v 2; "I groan" (21) restates v 8, "She . . . groans," and still other examples could be added. This echoing is frequently in the first person, contrasting with the third person of the original statement. The effect of this device is comparable to that of a composer's restatement, at the end of a movement, of the themes with which it began, modified and intensified. Following this coda the poem comes to a quiet close: "For many are my groans, and my heart is sick."

## II
## "The Lord became like an enemy"
### (2:1–22)

*aleph*    **2:1** How the Lord in his anger has treated Zion with contempt!

He has thrown down from heaven to earth    the glory of Israel.

He had no regard for his footstool    on the day of his wrath.

*beth*    2 The Lord consumed, unsparingly,    all the dwellings of Jacob.

He tore down, in his anger,    the fortresses of Judah.

He brought down to earth, he profaned,    her king and princes.

*gimel*    3 In fierce anger he lopped off    the horns of Israel.

He turned back his right hand    in the face of the enemy,

And he burned against Jacob like a fire    that consumes on every side.

*daleth*    4 He bent his bow like an enemy;    the sword hilt was in his right hand.

Like a foe &lt;he smote&gt; and slew    all those dear to her.

On the tents of Zion    he poured out his wrath like fire.

*he*    5 The Lord became an enemy;    he consumed Israel.

He consumed all her citadels;    he destroyed his fortresses.

In Judah he multiplied    moaning and mourning.

*waw*    6 He laid waste his covert like a garden;    he ruined his assembly.

The Lord made festival and sabbath    to be forgotten in Zion,

And in his fierce anger he poured contempt
on king and priest.

*zayin*    7 The Lord rejected his own altar;    he spurned
his sanctuary.
He gave over to the enemy    the walls of her
citadels.
They made a noise in the house of the LORD    as
though it were a feast day.

*heth*    8 The Lord planned to destroy    the wall of Zion.
He stretched out the line;    he did not relent
from slaughtering.
So he made rampart and wall mourn;    together
they languished.

*teth*    9 Her gates have sunk into the earth;    he
destroyed their bars.
Her king and her princes are among the
heathen;    there is no instruction;
Also her prophets find    no vision from the LORD.

*yod*    10 In silence they sit on the ground,    the elders of
Zion.
They put dirt on their heads;    they wear
sackcloth.
The young women of Jerusalem bow their
heads    to the ground.

*kaph*    11 My eyes are worn out with tears;    my bowels
churn.
My liver is poured out on the ground    at the
destruction of my people.
As the child and the baby were fainting    in the
streets of the city,

*lamed*    12 They said to their mothers,    "Where is grain
and wine?"
Fainting like wounded men    in the streets of the
city,
Breathing their last    in their mothers' laps.

*mem*    13 To what can I liken, to what compare you,    O
Jerusalem?
What likeness can I use to comfort you,    young
lady Zion?

For your ruin is as vast as the sea—     who could
    mend you?

*nun*    14 Your prophets saw visions for you     that were so
    much whitewash.
They did not lay bare your sin,     to make things
    better again,
But they saw for you oracles that were     empty
    deceptions.

*samekh*    15 All who pass along the road     clap hands at you;
They whistle and shake their heads     at
    Jerusalem.
"Is this the city they call     the perfection of
    beauty?"

*pe*    16 They open wide their mouths at you,     all your
    enemies;
They whistle and gnash their teeth;     they say,
    "We have consumed them!
Yes, this is the day we waited for!     We have seen
    it come to pass!"

*ayin*    17 The Lord has done what he planned;     he has
    carried out what he said he would,
What he commanded from olden times:     He
    tore down without sparing
And he made your enemies happy at your
    expense; He raised high the horns of your foes.

*sade*    18 Cry from the heart to the Lord,     O remorseful
    Zion!
Shed tears like a torrent     night and day.
Give yourself no relief!     Do not let your eyes be
    still!

*qof*    19 Arise, cry out at night,     as each watch begins.
Pour out your heart like water     before the face
    of the Lord.
Lift up your hands to him     for the lives of your
    children.

. . . . . . . . . . . . . . . . . . . . . . . . . . . . . . . . .

*resh*    20 "Look, Lord, and consider     to whom you have
    done this!

Should women eat what they bore,     the children
they have raised?
Should priest and prophet be slain     in the
sanctuary of the LORD?

*shin*     21 Out in the streets on the ground they lie,     boys
and old men.
My young men and women     have fallen by the
sword.
You killed them on the day of your
wrath,     slaughtering without mercy.

*taw*     22 You invited, as though to a festival,     men to
attack me from all sides,
So that, on the day of the Lord's wrath,     there
were none who escaped or got away.
My enemies have wiped them out—     the ones I
cherished and brought up."

# NOTES

**2** 1. *has treated . . . with contempt!* MT *yā'īb* is traditionally
taken as a denominative verb from *'āb* 'cloud' and translated "cover
with clouds" (so also Albrektson 1963 and others in modern times).
But this explanation of the *hapax legomenon* is suspiciously ad hoc,
and the meaning is not especially suited to this context, nor is
"beclouding" otherwise an image for punishment. Ehrlich (1914),
Rudolph (1962), and others have explained the word as related to
an Ar *'āba* 'to blame, revile', and translate: "How the Lord . . .
has disgraced Zion," which fits the context well. As an alternative
suggestion, one may propose (following in most respects McDaniel
1968b: 34–35) that the text be vocalized *yō'īb*, as if from a root
*\*w'b*, to which is related the noun *tō'ēbāh* ('abomination'; on the
derivation see W. F. Albright, *From the Stone Age to Christianity*
[Baltimore, 1957], 176 n. 45) and the denominative verb *t'b*. *yō'īb*
would be equal in sense to *tā'ēb*, as in Ps 106:40: "And the anger of
Yahweh was aroused at his people, and he treated with contempt
*(waytā'ēb)* his inheritance." Although *\*w'b* would be the original
root of *tō'ēbāh*, the *hiph'il hō'īb* might well be a denominative, a
back-formation from the noun; compare *hōdāh* from *tōdāh* as explained by W. F. Albright, "The Names 'Israel' and 'Judah' with

an Excursus on the Etymology of *tôdâh* and *tôrâh*," *Journal of Biblical Literature* 46 (1927): 151–85. Note that the Targum has a form of *qwṣ* 'despise'. See further the NOTE at 4:1.

*Zion.* "Daughter Zion"; see the INTRODUCTION.

*his footstool.* This is a reference to Zion or the temple as the symbol of the presence of God. It is not a reference to the Ark, as Albrektson claims (1963; though that may be the case in 1 Chr 28:2), since the Ark was not destroyed in 587 B.C., but much earlier, unless Jer 3:16 is a later interpolation in Jeremiah. The intention of this image seems to be to describe in a reverent, modest way the mode of God's presence: his throne is in heaven—that is, his dwelling is transcendent and remote—but he is nevertheless present in a special way in his temple, the place where his feet touch.

2. *dwellings.* Heb *neʾ ōt* is used of pastures, and also of the dwellings of men. The latter sense has been preferred here because the verb *billaʿ* 'he consumed' is used elsewhere in this chapter with buildings as its object (vv 5, 8), and because a reference to buildings seems to fit better in the context of the verse.

*Judah.* "Daughter Judah"; see the INTRODUCTION.

*her king and princes.* MT *mamlākāh weśārehā*, literally rendered as it stands, would be "a kingdom and its (her) princes." A translation "her king and princes" (so LXX) can be defended in various ways; for a detailed discussion, with references, see McDaniel 1968b: 35–36. The present writer prefers to suppose that the initial *m* of MT *mamlākāh* was originally an enclitic *mem* attached to the preceding verb, *ḥillēl* (on this particle, see the NOTE at 3:17), yielding the text *ḥillēl-m malkāh weśārehā*; cf. v 9b.

*profaned.* The use of "profaned" for *ḥillēl* is based on Ps 89:40 [ = 38E]; vv 39–46 [ = 38–45E] of the psalm resemble the present context in other respects also. Otherwise (as suggested to me by D. N. Freedman) one might translate "wounded."

3. *he lopped off the horns of Israel.* The meaning is "He destroyed all of Israel's proud strength." "Horn" as a metaphor for strength and pride is extremely frequent in the OT and occurs in other ancient Near Eastern literature as well; see Édouard Paul Dhorme, "L'Emploi métaphorique des noms de parties du corps en hébreu et en akkadien," *Revue biblique* 29 (1920): 465–506; 30 (1921): 374–99, 517–40; 31 (1922): 215–33, 489–547; 32 (1923):

185–212. Close parallels to the present passage are Jer 48:25; Ps 75:11 [ = 10E].

*his right hand.* The pronoun probably refers to Israel, not God. God destroys the "horn" of Israel in 3a, and here turns back Israel's right hand—both parts of the body, symbolic of strength, belong to Israel.

*like a fire.* The Hebrew has *kᵉʾēš lehābāh* 'like a fire of flame'. Since this wording seems to make the first colon too long, *lehābāh* is to be deleted, either as an addition made because the construct phrase was such a frequently used idiom (e.g., Isa 4:5) or as a variant reading that has been incorporated into the text (cf. the NOTE on 5:5).

4. The text is suspect at several points. *niṣṣāb yᵉmīnō*, literally, "his right hand (fem.) is stationed" (masc. adj.), can scarcely be correct. If *kᵉṣār* 'like a foe' is added to the end of line 1, the line is made rather long, and line 2 is too short; but if it is put with line 2, the result is an impossible "like a foe and he slew." The present translation is based on understanding *niṣṣāb* as the noun "(sword) hilt," as in Judg 3:22, which was suggested to the present writer by J. Rimbach, and on restoring a *b* ("in"; lost by haplography?) before *yᵉmīnō*. For parallels to the picture of God as a warrior who draws a bow and wields a sword (not simultaneously, of course!) see Ps 7:14 [ = 13E]; Zech 9:13; cf. Isa 41:2; Ps 37:14. In the second line *kᵉṣār* 'like a foe' is a good parallel to *kᵉʾōyēb*, but a verb has dropped out after it, perhaps *hikkāh* 'he smote', to judge from the association of *hikkāh* and *hāraq* in Isa 27:7 and Ps 136:17–18. If *hikkāh* or a verb of similar meaning is inserted at this point, the resulting line exhibits a syntactic pattern common in Lamentations; see the NOTE on 1:6.

*all those dear to her.* Literally, "those desirable to the eye," used elsewhere of people (Ezek 24:16) and of precious things (1 Kgs 20:6). Compare the COMMENT on 1:11.

*Zion.* "Daughter Zion"; see the INTRODUCTION.

5. *his.* The MT gives the feminine suffix with "citadels," and the masculine with "fortresses."

*Judah.* "Daughter Judah"; see the INTRODUCTION. To 5c compare "Lamentation over the Destruction of Sumer and Ur," ANET, p. 617, lines 361–62: "The desolate city—in its midst there was uttered (nothing but) laments (and) dirges." So also p. 619, lines 486–87.

6. The first line is translated here as literally as possible. If the MT is correct, which is most doubtful, the point might be that Yahweh laid waste his "covert," that is, the temple (cf. Ps 27:5) and ruined his (place of) festal assembly (mŏᶜᵃdŏ; Morris Jastrow, ZAW 15 [1895]: "Threni 2:6ᵃ", 287 compares Ps 74:4 for this meaning of mŏᶜēd). The Targum already recognized this sense in the present verse. One can point to passages likening the ruin of a people to the ruining of a vineyard, notably Isa 5:5–6, also Jer 5:10; 12:10; and the verb šiḥḥēt, which is used here (or hiphᶜil hišḥīt), occurs in such contexts. Even so, this interpretation is obviously forced at several points, and is retained here only for want of something better. Most commentators have suggested some sort of emendation, often employing in some way the ambiguous evidence of the versions, but of the many proposals, none seems thoroughly convincing. Albrektson (who defends the MT, 1963) and McDaniel (1968b: 36–38) treat the passage at length and refer to previous discussions.

7. her citadels. The pronoun "her" is retained here on the supposition that it refers to Zion (cf. v 6). An emendation to "his" citadels produces consistency in the verse, but would make it necessary to explain what are the "citadels of Yahweh." Citadels (ʾarmᵉnŏt) are not elsewhere said to belong to Yahweh.

as though it were a feast day. Compare Hos 12:10 [ = 9E].

8. Zion. "Daughter Zion"; see the INTRODUCTION.

He stretched out the line. Stretching a line is the action of a builder, done to mark straight lines. It is occasionally used, as here, as a metaphor for divine judgment. It is not completely clear how a phrase from the vocabulary of building becomes a synonym for destruction, but it may be that the idea is of a strict, predetermined measure from which God will not deviate; cf. 2 Kgs 21:13; Isa 28:17; 34:11. Brunet (1966: 189–98) reaches a similar conclusion in an extensive treatment of the figure; he compares the modern use of a balance as a symbol of justice.

rampart and wall. Compare Isa 26:1.

9. The MT has another verb: "he destroyed and shattered her gate bars." Since this makes a rather long second colon, it is possible that the MT is a conflation of variant readings, as occasionally occurs elsewhere in this book (see the NOTE on 5:5). So also Gordis

1967: ad loc. There seems to be no decisive reason for choosing one reading in preference to the other.

10. *In silence.* Heb *dāmam* means "be silent" in some passages, but in others it probably means "to wail, mourn"; here, as in some other contexts, either meaning is appropriate. For a summary of the problem, with references to extended treatments, see McDaniel 1968b: 38–40.

11. *the destruction of my people.* Literally, "the breaking of (the daughter of [see the INTRODUCTION]) my people," an expression that has its closest parallels in Jeremiah (6:14; 8:11, 21; cf. 14:17). Also similar are Amos 6:6; Isa 30:26.

12. *and wine.* Budde and others have objected to "and wine" on the ground that little children would not have asked for an alcoholic beverage, but this is hypercritical.

13. *liken.* I read *'e^ce̓rōk*, with the Vg *(cui comparabo te)*, for MT *'a̓c̓īdēk* 'testify', as proposed by Meinhold 1895. The pattern of synonymous verbs, joined by *waw*, sharing an object, is a favorite one in the book; compare for example, 3:2. *'ārak* is associated with *dāmāh* also in Isa 40:18 and Ps 89:7 [ = 6E].

*Jerusalem.* "Daughter Jerusalem"; see the INTRODUCTION.

*young lady Zion.* "Virgin daughter Zion"; see the INTRODUCTION.

14. *so much whitewash.* Heb *šāw̓ w^etāpēl*, literally, "emptiness and whitewash," as applied to visions by false prophets, is best explained by the more extended figure in Ezek 13:10–16, where prophets of peace are compared to men who would whitewash over a rickety wall; cf. also Ezek 22:28.

*oracles that were empty deceptions. maś̓ōt šāw̓ ūmaddūḥīm* is as it stands a construct chain, perfectly acceptable Hebrew in itself, but such as to make it hard to read this line as 3 + 2 *(qinah* meter). Hence Budde 1898 (followed recently by Kraus 1968) wished to repoint the first word as absolute *maśśā̓ōt*, and take the following words as appositives. This charge makes the sense of the first colon too flat, however. Rudolph (1962) proposes emending to (otherwise unattested) *maśśā̓ōt* 'deceptions'. It seems better to retain the MT and alter one's metrical theory to fit.

15. The MT adds, after "perfection of beauty," another epithet, "The joy of the whole earth," which makes the line too long. Since *šeyyō̓m^erū* 'they call' or 'of which they said' is necessary

to the syntax, one is compelled to choose between the two epithets for Zion. "The perfection of beauty" occurs as an epithet for Tyre (Ezek 27:3), and almost identical epithets are used of the king of Tyre (Ezek 28:12) and of Zion (Ps 50:2). "The joy of the whole earth" recurs (in only slightly different form) as a title of Mount Zion in Ps 48:3 [ = 2E]; cf. also Jer 51:41. It may be that the MT is a conflation of variant versions of the line; there is no firm basis for preferring one reading to the other.

17. On the horn metaphor, see the NOTE at v 3.

18. Translation of the first line is based on conjectural emendation of the MT. Literally rendered, the MT is "Their heart cried out to the Lord, the wall of Zion" ("Daughter Zion," see the INTRODUCTION), which is obviously unsatisfactory. For $ṣā^caq$ (perfect) read $ṣa^{c a}qī$ (fem. sing. imperative), as many have proposed. *libbām* is understood as "(from) the heart," which involves recognizing the *mem* as enclitic or perhaps adverbial (cf. McDaniel 1968b: 203–4). For *hōmat* read <ni> *ḥḥemet* ('repentant', 'remorseful'; *niphᶜal* participle fem. from *nāḥam*) on the supposition that the correct text was lost under the influence of v 8. For a very similar pattern in a poetic line compare Isa 52:2, "O captive daughter Zion (*šᵉbīyyāh bat ṣiyyōn*)" and Jer 46:19; 48:18; Zech 2:11 [ = 7E], all with *yōšebet bat* X (place name).

*relief. pūgat* is either a case in which the feminine ending -*t* has been retained in the absolute singular or a construct in a construction of the *simḥat baqqāṣīr* type.

19. *Pour out your heart.* The meaning of *šipkī . . . libbēk*, which occurs only twice in the OT (here and Ps 62:9 [ = 8E]) is apparently very much like that of the common English expression, hence the sense is "give expression to your innermost thoughts and feelings." Compare also 1 Sam 1:15. "Like water" is a stock simile used with the verb "pour out"; cf. Deut 12:16, 24; 15:23; Ps 79:3; Hos 5:10.

The MT adds a fourth line at the end of this verse: "Who fainted from hunger at every street corner." In the opinion of most commentators, it is an addition, a mosaic of bits from vv 11c, 12b, and 4:1b. The reference to "your children" in the previous line provided the peg for the addition. It is the only one of the four lines that can be omitted without raising new problems within the verse.

20. *they have raised.* The *hapax legomenon ṭippūḥīm* and the related verb *ṭippaḥtī* in v 22 are translated as having to do with child rearing since this reading fits the contexts and is supported by an Akkadian cognate *ṭepū* as well; cf. W. von Soden, "Zum akkadischen Wörterbuch, 6–14," *Orientalia* n.s. 16 (1947): 77–78.

To 20c and 21a and b, which speak of the dead in the sanctuary and the streets, compare "Lamentation over the Destruction of Ur," *ANET*, p. 459: "In its lofty gates, where they were wont to promenade, dead bodies were lying about; / In its boulevards, where the feasts were celebrated, scattered they lay. / In all its streets, where they were wont to promenade, dead bodies were lying about; / In its places, where the festivities of the land took place, the people lay in heaps."

22. *men to attack me from all sides.* Whatever the correct rendering of Jeremiah's *māgōr missābīb* in each of its occurrences (Jer 6:25; 20:3, 10; 46:5; 49:29; also Ps 31:14 [ = 13E]), and whatever its relation to the present passage may be, it seems best not to translate *mᵉgūray missābīb* here "my terrors on every side" (so the RSV and similarly many others), since it seems that men are referred to—to have "terrors" invited to a festival would involve a mixture of metaphors not typical of Hebrew poetry. "Attackers" is suggested by the context and by the meaning of *gūr* in several biblical passages (see KB³, s.v. *gūr* II and especially Job 18:19) and also perhaps by Ug *gr* in *CTA* 14 ( = Krt) 110–11: *wgr.nn.ʿrm*. Or one might propose a meaning "Those who lie in wait for me/ besiege me," based on *gūr* I, "to abide"; note that in Ps 59:4 [ = 3E] the parallel to *yāgūrū ʿālay* is *ʾārᵉbū lᵉnapšī*. The pointing of the MT is probably incorrect, but the correct vocalization is uncertain; perhaps best is *mᵉgōray*, as a contracted form of an assumed *polel* participle *\*mᵉgōrᵉray* (cf. GKC, para. 72cc). Rudolph (1962) also points thus but translates "those who terrify me," which gives good sense. For a fuller discussion see McDaniel 1968b: 42–44.

# COMMENT

In externals the second Lamentation is very much like the first. It is an alphabetic acrostic poem of three-line stanzas, and only the first line of each stanza is made to conform to the acrostic pattern.

The only formal difference is that, contrary to the normal order of the Hebrew alphabet, *pe* precedes *ayin* (as also in chapters 3 and 4) in the Masoretic Text; see the INTRODUCTION for the reading of 4QLam[a], which also has the reverse order, apparently paralleled in some ancient Hebrew inscriptions. The reason for this variation escapes me. The meter is predominantly of the *qinah* type (see the INTRODUCTION). The date seems to be the same as that for chapter 1: shortly after the fall of Jerusalem in 587 B.C.

In other respects, however, chapter 2 contrasts with chapter 1. Here there is less of the personification of Zion, and only at the very end (vv 20–22) does she speak for herself. For the most part it is the poet who speaks of what happened to Zion, or who addresses the city. Moreover, the structure of the chapter is determined not so much by a psychological progression, as was true of the first poem, but primarily by a logical sequence of material. Although this order is not strictly maintained in every detail, in general this second poem may be outlined as follows:

A.  Since it is Yahweh who destroyed Zion . . .

    1.  Yahweh himself destroyed Zion, vv 1–9a

    2.  How and why Yahweh destroyed Zion, vv 9b–17

        a.  The destruction and its cause described by the poet, vv 9b–12

        b.  The poet continues, but addresses Zion directly, vv 13–16

        c.  The theme restated: Yahweh has destroyed Zion, v 17

B.  Therefore cry out to Yahweh! vv 18–19

C.  Zion's anguished appeal, vv 20–22

The main point of this chapter is that it was Yahweh himself who destroyed city and people, and the writer seldom strays very far from this idea. Even when Zion herself finally appears and appeals to God, her words are not so much a prayer for help as a helpless restatement of the principal theme. The agent of destruction, the Lord (or Yahweh; cf. the NOTE on 1:14), is introduced in the very first line, and the name is given unusual prominence by the word order of the Hebrew: it is separated from the verb and placed first in the second colon. The exact sense of line 1 is unfortunately uncertain (see the NOTE), but the following lines express clear and vivid ideas. The extent of the catastrophe is described as a fall from the sky—traditional in Hebrew as the absolute height—to earth, the absolute depth (cf. Prov 25:3: "The sky for height and the earth for depth," and many other passages). Weiser (1962) sees here an allusion to the mythological motif of a fall from heaven (Isa 14:12; Ezek 28:17), but that is perhaps overspecific. Next it is the mystery of the divine wrath that is brought into prominence: Yahweh paid no attention to the fact that Zion was his own "footstool," his own elect city and temple, sign of his presence with his people. This paradox is restated, directly and indirectly, throughout the chapter. This was a "day of the Lord's anger" (cf. the COMMENT on 1:12), when the divine anger was directed against his own people.

In succeeding verses (2–5) God is depicted as a mighty warrior, pitiless in his anger. He has struck both the buildings (2a, b; 5a, b) and the people of Zion. Her king and princes, who were sacred persons because of special closeness to him, he has brought low and defiled (2c). Three familiar metaphors follow: Yahweh has "lopped off the horns of Israel," that is, has destroyed her strength and pride (see the NOTE); he has turned back his (Israel's; see the NOTE) "right hand," a common symbol of prowess (often of God, but also, as here, of men, e.g., Ps 137:5); and his anger has burned like fire against Jacob.

The following verse (4) makes the picture of God as warrior still more explicit. On the history of this conception of God, see P. Miller, "God the Warrior," *Interpretation* 19 (1965): 39–46; and F. M. Cross, Jr., "The Divine Warrior in Israel's Early Cult," in *Biblical Motifs: Origins and Transformations*, ed. Alexander Altmann (Cambridge, Mass., 1966), 11–30. With bow and sword (conjectural—see the NOTE), he killed all those dear to mother Israel. The tendency in Israelite thought to ignore secondary causes and think of Yahweh as the cause of all calamity (cf. Amos 3:6) could not appear more unmistakably! After a reiteration of the statement that Yahweh destroyed the city's fortifications, there is a brief allusion to the people's reaction: moaning and mourning were abundant ("moaning and mourning" is an attempt to reflect the obviously intentional assonance of the Heb *taʾᵃnīyyāh waʾᵃnīyyāh*, derivatives of the same root; this pair is also found in Isa 29:2).

In verses 6 and 7 the dominant idea is that touched on already in v 1: Yahweh has destroyed what was sacred to himself, sacred objects (altar, sanctuary, temple), people (king and priest), and institutions (festival and sabbath) alike. The enemy was allowed to raise an unholy din in the temple, so that it sounded as though a kind of witches' sabbath were being celebrated.

Lest there be any misconception, it is made clear that Yahweh did all this, not through inadvertence, but deliberately; he planned it (8); he stretched out the line, the deliberate act of a man planning a project (see the NOTE); and he did not change his mind. Mention of the walls and ramparts constitutes a bridge to the next stanza. Rather often the author deliberately "syncopates," that is, he sees to it that divisions of thought and formal divisions do not always coincide (cf., e.g., vv 11–12; 3:12–13; and the beginning of the COMMENT on chap. 3). "Her gates have sunk into the earth" is probably meant as a literal statement, to which may be compared "The Curse of Agade" (Cooper's translation), 168: "The doors of all the city-gates of the land lay dislodged in the dirt" (*The Curse of Agade* [Baltimore and London, 1983]). If not, one might suppose that the "gates" were personified here, like the "mourning" walls of the preceding line (cf. 1:4), and then "sunk into the earth" would recall what is said elsewhere of persons; to have one's feet sink (*ṭābaʿ*) into mud (Ps 69:3 [ = 69:2E], 15 [ = 69:14E] Jer 38:22) is a figure for being in great distress.

With the next line (9b) the attention shifts for a time away from Yahweh and toward the city herself, especially the people. All of the most important people are either gone or not functioning: king, princes, priests—it is they who would normally have supplied the "instruction" (*tōrāh*)—and prophets. (Cf. Ezek 7:26; Mic 3:6; Ps 74:9; 1 Sam 3:1.) The elders mourn for Zion with typical mourning rites, as though for a dead person. (On the whole passage, see Jahnow 1923: 7.) They sit on the ground. This traditional attitude (cf. Ezek 26:16; Job 2:12; 2 Sam 13:31; Josh 7:6) expresses humiliation, the earth being symbolic of lowness. In this pose also a man was in direct contact with dirt, a recurring image of mortality. If the verb *dāmam* is correctly translated here (see the NOTE), the elders keep silence for a period—another customary mourning observance, on which see Lohfink 1962. They put dirt on their heads, an age-old mourning gesture attested already in Ugaritic texts (from about the fourteenth century B.C.). This was an acting out of "Dust thou art and unto dust shalt thou return." (On dust as metaphor in the OT, see Hillers, "Dust: Some Aspects of Old Testament Imagery," in *Love and Death,* ed. J. Marks and R. M. Good [New Haven, 1987], 105–9.) For parallels see Josh 7:6; 1 Sam 4:12; 2 Sam 1:2; 15:32; Ezek 27:30; Job 2:12; 42:6; Neh 9:1. El performs this rite in a Ugaritic myth (*CTA* 5 = *UT* 67 vi 14–16); for an Akkadian parallel see *CAD,* s.v. *eperu,* p. 187. They put on sackcloth. The virgins let their heads sink to the earth. The specific mention of "old men" and "young women" ("virgins") as the two classes that mourn is perhaps to be accounted for as a merism, that is, these are the two opposite limits of the population, and the sense is that the whole population mourns. Alternatively, as maintained above (on 1:4), mention of "virgins" in such a context may derive from an old literary tradition, the source of which is the myth of the mourning Virgin goddess.

In v 11, the poet speaks of his own consuming grief. As frequently in the Old Testament, the bowels are regarded as the body's organ involved in intense emotion. The "pouring out" of the liver is not elsewhere mentioned in the MT as it stands, but Ps 7:6 [ = 5E] is probably to be read "He sets my liver (not *kᵉbōdī* 'my honor') in the dirt," which would be a close parallel to the present verse.

The famine, which struck the little children especially, is depicted in a dramatic vignette. Starving children ask their mothers for bread and wine, but there is none, and they faint in the streets, or expire in their mothers' laps.

The description of Zion's misery continues, but takes a new turn as the poet for a time addresses the city directly (vv 13–16). This shift prepares the way for the imperatives addressed to Zion in the next major section, beginning with v 18. The questions of v 13 are rhetorical, for there is no adequate comparison for the present wretchedness of Zion. (It is not clear just why finding a comparison for Zion would comfort her; one explanation [Jahnow 1923; Rudolph 1962] is that a person will feel better if he is shown that his case is not unique, but this view is rather unconvincing.) Even when the author goes on to use a simile—"vast as the sea"—it is actually another way of saying the same thing, since the sea is the traditional element for expressing size and length. Already in a

Ugaritic text (CTA 23 = *UT* 52 33–35) El's "hand" is "long as the sea" (cf. Jean Nougayrol, *Ugaritica* 5 [Paris, 1969], text 3 RS 24 245, line 2). According to Job 11:9, no one can take the measure of God: "its breadth is greater than the sea" (cf. Isa 48:18; Ps 104:25). If a thing is beyond the sea, it is as unreachable as something in the sky (Deut 30:12–13). Zion is shattered totally, beyond repair.

From speaking of Jerusalem's present misery, the writer turns for a single stanza (v 14) to consideration of its cause. The people had sinned, yet the prophets, those who supposedly had the most spiritual and moral insight, did not lay it bare but painted it over with oracles of "Peace, peace" (see the NOTE on "whitewash"). Israel's destruction was not inevitable. Had her sin been made open and had she repented (the idea is implicit, not expressed in the terse poetic line), she might have enjoyed good times again. (On this meaning of Heb *šūb šᵉbūt* cf., e.g., Deut 30:3; Ezek 16:53; Hos 6:11; Amos 9:14.)

After this single backward look the poem returns to the present misery, which is depicted by a familiar figure. All those who pass by Jerusalem express their contempt of her in her ruinous state (cf. 1 Kgs 9:8; Jer 18:16; 19:8; 49:17; 50:13; Ezek 5:14; 36:34; Zeph 2:15; Ps 80:13 [ = 12E]). Her proud title, "perfection of beauty," hers by right of being Yahweh's chosen city, is now flung in her teeth. This passage is reminiscent of the lines from Ps 42:4, 11 [ = 3, 10E]: "My foes revile me, saying to me, 'Where is your God?' " Adding to the intolerable nature of what the enemies say is the fact that they are, even if unconscious of it, doing God's work. The following verse (17) makes this paradox explicit, but it is there already in the language of the enemies. Their "We have consumed" echoes "The Lord consumed" of vv 2 and 5; their "day" recalls "the day of his wrath," v 1.

The first main section of the lament closes with a return to the major theme with which the poem began: Yahweh has done what he planned. With a certain hyperbole it is even asserted that Israel's destruction was his purpose from "olden times."

The call for Zion to pray heaps up expressive devices to make it clear that her appeal to God must be both sincere and extraordinary. She is to cry "from the heart" (see the NOTE at v 18) and to "pour out her heart" (v 19), shedding tears continually, night and day. The last phrase, "for the lives of your children," leads into the prayer itself, which is about "children" in two senses. In the first place, the slaughtered citizens of Jerusalem are regarded as the children of the personified Zion, who weeps over them like Rachel. In a more literal sense, it is the actual little children who are uppermost in the poet's mind; they are mentioned first and last.

Zion's prayer does not contain any explicit petition, only that Yahweh should look on: "Consider to whom you have done this!" It comes close to being a reproach to Yahweh, or if not that, then at least a strong appeal to his compassion. Granted that Jerusalem had sinned, the actual conquest brought ghastly extremes of suffering, which seemed to those involved to be out of proportion to any guilt of the sufferers. This view appears most clearly in the case of the children and the mothers, who suffered not only starvation but loss of all humanity. References to cannibalism in the time of siege frequently appear in the Old Testament and other ancient Near Eastern literature; see the COMMENT on 1:11. Also revolting to ordinary human religious feeling is the idea that men of God should be killed right in the sanctuary, where they ministered (20c). In the lines rendered "Should women eat. . . . Should priest and prophet . . ." the imperfect verbs could also be rendered as incredulous questions: "Can it be that women eat . . . ?" and so on.

None has escaped. Old men and boys, young men and women lie in the streets, unburied. As in v 17, the poet puts Yahweh, the ultimate and in his mind real cause, in the foreground; only at the very end (22c) do the human enemies receive notice. The combination of words "the day of your wrath" and "slaughtered (*ṭābaḥtā*)" with "as though to a festival (*mōʿēd*)" suggests that the writer is alluding to the picture elaborated most fully in Isaiah 34: the day of God's wrath is a grisly banquet at which men are slaughtered like animals of sacrifice. Note that vocabulary similar to that of v 21 recurs in Ps 44:23 [ = 22E] and Jer 12:3, where the comparison to sacrificial animals is explicit.

The human agents of Yahweh's wrath are brought into the picture at the very end. Yahweh invited them to gather on all sides of the city and lay siege to it. Since they encircled it, there was no chance for escape (cf. Jer 50:29, "Encamp against her on all sides; let no one get away"). Like the first poem, so this one also ends on a low, pathetic tone, as mother Zion mourns once again the loss of her children.

# III
## Everyman
## (3:1–66)

| | | |
|---|---|---|
| *aleph* | **3:**1 | "I am the man who has seen hardship    under the rod of his anger. |
| *aleph* | 2 | He led and guided me—    into darkness and gloom, |
| *aleph* | 3 | He turned his hand against me above all,    again and again, all day. |
| *beth* | 4 | He wore out my flesh and skin;    he broke my bones. |
| *beth* | 5 | He besieged and encircled me    with poverty and hardship. |
| *beth* | 6 | He made me sit in the dark    like those long dead. |
| *gimel* | 7 | He shut me in so I cannot escape;    he put me in heavy chains. |
| *gimel* | 8 | Even when I cry out and ask for help,    he shuts out my prayer. |
| *gimel* | 9 | He has blocked up my ways with cut stones;    he has made my paths crooked. |
| *daleth* | 10 | He is a lurking bear to me,    a lion in hiding: |
| *daleth* | 11 | He turned me aside and tore me apart.    He made me desolate. |
| *daleth* | 12 | He bent his bow and set me up    as a target for his arrows. |
| *he* | 13 | He shot me in the vitals    with shafts from his quiver. |
| *he* | 14 | I have become a joke to all my people;    all day long they mock me in song. |
| *he* | 15 | He gave me my fill of bitter things;    he sated me with wormwood. |

| | |
|---|---|
| *waw* | 16 He ground my teeth in the gravel;     he trampled me into the dust. |
| *waw* | 17 I despaired of having peace;     I forgot everything good. |
| *waw* | 18 I thought, 'My lasting hope in the Lord     has perished.' |
| *zayin* | 19 I remember my miserable wandering,     the wormwood and poison. |
| *zayin* | 20 Within myself I surely remember     and am despondent. |
| *zayin* | 21 Yet one thing I will keep in mind     which will give me hope: |
| *heth* | 22 The Lord's mercy is surely not at an end,     nor is his pity exhausted. |
| *heth* | 23 It is new every morning.     Great is your faithfulness! |
| *heth* | 24 The Lord is my portion, I tell myself,     therefore I will hope. |
| *teth* | 25 The Lord is good to the person who waits for him,     to the person who seeks him. |
| *teth* | 26 It is good that a man hope in quiet     for the Lord's deliverance. |
| *teth* | 27 It is good for a man     that he bear the yoke in his youth. |
| *yod* | 28 Let him sit in silence by himself     when it is heavy on him. |
| *yod* | 29 Let him put his mouth in the dirt—     maybe there is hope. |
| *yod* | 30 Let him turn his cheek to the one who strikes him;     let him have his fill of disgrace. |
| *kaph* | 31 Because the Lord does not reject forever     . . . . . . . |
| *kaph* | 32 Because after he has afflicted he will have pity,     out of his abounding mercy; |

*kaph*    33 Because he does not deliberately torment
              men,    or afflict them

*lamed*   34 By crushing under foot    all the prisoners of the
              earth,

*lamed*   35 By denying a man justice    before the Most
              High,

*lamed*   36 By twisting a man's case    without the Lord
              seeing.

*mem*    37 Who was it who 'spoke and it was  done'?    It
              was the Lord who gave the command.

*mem*    38 Both bad and good take place    at the command
              of the Most High.

*mem*    39 Why should a man complain over his
              punishment,    as long as he is still alive?

*nun*    40 Let us rather test and examine our ways,    and
              return to the Lord.

*nun*    41 Let us lift our heart along with our hands    to
              God above."

*nun*    42 "We have rebelled and disobeyed.    You have not
              forgiven.

*samekh*  43 You have enveloped us in anger and pursued
              us;    you have slain without sparing.

*samekh*  44 You have wrapped yourself in cloud    so no
              prayer could get through.

*samekh*  45 You make us a despised off-scouring    among the
              nations.

*pe*     46 All our enemies    open their mouths wide at us.
*pe*     47 We have been through panic and pit,    wreck
              and ruin."

*pe*     48 "My eyes run with streams of tears    at the ruin
              of my people.

*ayin*    49 My eyes will stream without stopping,    without
              relief,

*ayin*      50 Until the Lord looks out from above     to see.

*ayin*      51 The affliction done to me,     has consumed my eyes."

*sade*      52 "Those who are my enemies for no reason     hunted me like a bird.

*sade*      53 They shut me tight in a pit     and threw stones at me.

*sade*      54 Waters came over my head.     I said, 'I am cut off.'

*qof*      55 Out of the lowest pit, O Lord,     I call your name.

*qof*      56 Hear my voice—Do not close your ears—     to relieve me, to save me!

*qof*      57 Be near when I call you;     tell me not to be afraid.

*resh*      58 Lord, be on my side in this struggle;     redeem my life.

*resh*      59 Lord, see the injustice I suffer;     uphold my cause.

*resh*      60 See how they took revenge on me,     plotted against me.

*shin*      61 Listen to how they reproach me, Lord,     how they plot against me.

*shin*      62 The speech and the thoughts of my enemies     are against me all day.

*shin*      63 Look, in everything they do     I am the butt of their mockery.

*taw*      64 Give them, O Lord, what they have coming,     for what their hands have done.

*taw*      65 Give them anguish of heart,     as your curse on them!

*taw*      66 May you pursue them in anger     and wipe them out from under the Lord's heaven!"

# NOTES

**3** 2. This is one of the lines in which the first colon contains two verbs joined by a *waw*-consecutive (see the NOTE on 1:6 above). The second colon typically (not always) contains elements that modify both verbs. Hence the effect is to separate sharply between the verbal predicates and the subsequent modifiers; the caesura seems to be emphasized. Begrich (1933–34: 174–75) lists similar examples mostly in the Psalms (most of his, however, do not involve a *waw*-consecutive form). He accounts for the construction as being due to the necessity to fill up the line when it consisted of a single sentence, but that seems not to have been the only motive.

*gloom.* Literally, "not light," probably best understood as a compound of negative plus noun, a formation sufficiently common in Hebrew; cf. *l' kh* 'not-strength', 1:6.

3. *turned his hand against me.* A. Fitzgerald has observed that the verb *hāpak* is not elsewhere combined with *yād* 'hand' except in cases in which the turning of a chariot is spoken of, which obviously does not apply to the present case. Hence he would understand the text quite differently, as "He reverses his love all the day"; see "Hebrew *yd* = 'Love' and 'Beloved,'" *CBQ* 29 (1967): 368–69. In my opinion, the Hebrew phrase he would substitute is just as unparalleled as the MT (since Ps 105:25, which he cites, is not a good parallel), and his interpretation is more forced than the traditional understanding of the Hebrew text.

5. "Besieged" is a somewhat free rendering of *bānah* ('he built'); here, in combination with *wayyaqqap* ('and he encircled'), the verb seems to convey the idea of "to build up around, wall in" (cf. 2 Kgs 6:14).

*poverty.* Reading (as also NJV ) *rē'š* ( = *rēš*, cf. Prov 6:11; 30:8) for MT *rō'š* 'poison'. The combination of concrete and abstract in MT "venom and hardship" seems unacceptable.

11. *tore me apart.* Since the Heb *waypašš<sup>e</sup>hēnī* occurs only here, and the translation relies on the Syriac and the Targum, it is not certain that the image of God as a predatory animal continues into this verse especially, because *d<sup>e</sup>rākay sōrēr* is also of uncertain meaning.

13. *in the vitals.* Literally, "in my kidneys," as the most vulnerable and sensitive target; cf. Job 16:13.

14. A Sebir, or ancient conjecture by Jewish textual scholars, gives "all peoples" instead of "all my people," and this plural turns up elsewhere in the textual tradition. It seems to arise from a desire to interpret the poem as referring to the whole people, which the MT makes difficult at this point.

17. *I despaired*, etc. My translation here follows the suggestion of Horace Hummel, "Enclitic Men in Early Northwest Semitic, Especially in Hebrew," *Journal of Biblical Literature* 76 (1957): 105, who recognizes in the initial *m* of *miššālōm* an enclitic *mem*, which should be attached to the preceding verb. *šālōm* then becomes the direct object of *zānaḥ*, which is usually transitive.

18. *lasting hope*. Hebrew "my enduring and my hope" is taken to be a hendiadys.

19. *I remember*. The imperative of the MT (*zᵉkor*) has seemed difficult to many commentators in this context, because the change in the speaker's attitude seems to begin only later, at v 21. Some have preferred to read here a noun, *zēker*, or to take the MT not as an imperative but as the infinitive *zᵉkōr*, yielding a translation, "The memory of my miserable wandering is wormwood," and so on. The present translation is based on context and the reading of the LXX, which gives a first-person form, "I remember." Since the Greek translator does not ordinarily depart from the text before him in such matters, it is best to assume that his Hebrew text had either *zākartī* or possibly *zākōr ᵃnī*, an infinitive absolute followed by an independent personal pronoun indicating the subject. Interpretation of this line is to some extent tied up with the question of how one reads v 20; see the NOTE that follows.

*my miserable wandering*. Compare the NOTE on *mᵉrūdehā* at 1:7.

20. *am despondent*. Reading the *qere* *wᵉtāšōaḥ*, from the root *šḥḥ*. For close parallels, see Pss 42:6, 7, 12 [ = 5, 6, 11E]; 43:5. (The *ketib* implies *tāšīaḥ*, evidently a *hiphʿil* of *šwḥ*; this form is unparalleled, and it is not clear what sense it would have.) The tradition that the MT at this point embodies a *Tiqqun Sopherim* raises a minor problem concerning this otherwise unproblematic line, but the difficulty has been exacerbated by confusion on the part of commentators. The *Tiqqune Sopherim* ("corrections of the scribes") are changes made in the Hebrew text at an early stage, deliberately, for dogmatic reasons. These slight emendations were

intended to eliminate expressions that were thought to be too an-
thropomorphic or otherwise inconsistent with the dignity of God.
Where tradition records that the scribes deliberately changed the
text, there is, of course, a strong presumption that the existing MT
is wrong. In the case here, however, such a conclusion is probably
not correct. Ample details on this subject, and a discussion of the
present case, may be found in McCarthy 1981: 120–23 and
Barthélemy 1986. McCarthy offers only a very tentative suggestion
for the origin of the tradition that there is a *tiqqun* at this point,
and one may doubt that there was any ancient tradition regarding
the original reading. If the text has in fact been altered at some
point, the change is far from obvious, for none of the conjectures
advanced about the "original" reading are convincingly grammatical and idiomatic, whereas MT Qre has strong support from the
parallels cited, Pss 42:6, 7, 12 [ = 5, 6, 11E]; 43:5, and (disregard-
ing the *ketib-qere* complications) is supported by the versions as
well.

22. *is surely not at an end.* With many commentators, I am
reading *tammū* for MT *tām^enū*. The Targum implies *tammū* as the
reading of its Vorlage, and the Syriac may do so, though Albrektson
(1963) questions the latter point. The two *kī^'s* are asseverative, not
causal; "surely" is intended to reflect their force. On this particle
see references in McDaniel 1968b: 210 n. 2. McDaniel's interpretation of the verse is noteworthy (pp. 212–14). He vocalizes *kī lō'*
*timmānū kī lō' kīlū* and translates "The mercies of Yahweh are
innumerable! Verily, his compassions are immeasurable," but the
attempt to defend the MT is perhaps more ingenious than convincing.

25. *the person.* The MT's consonantal text, *qww*, seems to stand
for a singular (*\*qōwēw* from *\*qōwēhū*); the vocalization suggests a
plural. The parallel word, *nepeš*, is singular and favors the singular
reading, though this is scarcely conclusive evidence.

26. The MT of the first colon is slightly corrupt, and cannot be
explained as it stands. There is widespread agreement that the
sense of the line must be approximately that given here, and that
the roots *yḥl* 'wait' and *dūm/dāmam* 'be silent' must have stood in
the original in some form. Albrektson (1963: 146–48) has a thor-
ough discussion of previous suggestions. The present translation
presupposes loss of a *kī* and several lesser errors; the original was
perhaps *ṭōb <kī> yaḥīl dūmām*.

27. Some Hebrew manuscripts, some Greek ones, and the Vg have "from his youth." Since this is a much more common expression in the OT than "in (his, etc.) youth," it seems preferable to retain the MT here, as the less common expression.

28. *is heavy.* The rare verb *nāṭal* otherwise means "to lift, bear" in the OT, but the related noun *nēṭel* means "weight" in Prov 27:3 (parallel to *kōbed*), and the verb *nṭal* in Syriac means "to be heavy." For *nāṭal ʿal* compare *kābēd ʿal.* This proposal eliminates the need to press *nāṭal* here to mean "he (Yahweh) lifted up and laid on," as is usually done.

31. The text is too short, something having been omitted in the course of its transmission, but it is impossible to supply the deficiency with anything approaching certainty or probability. "His servants" (Lowth cited in Rudolph, 1962) and "mankind" (Rudolph 1962) have been proposed as objects.

34. To fit the acrostic, the poet makes each line begin with an infinitive preceded by *l.* By itself this Hebrew construction does not make a sentence, and the infinitives must depend on some finite verb. Many commentators and translators have construed the infinitives as objects of *ʾᵃdōnāy lōʾ rāʾāh* in 36, which is translated either as a question ("When one crushes under foot . . . did not the Lord see it?") or as a statement (cf. Rudolph's "When one crushes, . . . the Lord does not mind it!"; cf. the NRSV's "When all, . . . does the Lord not see it?"). But these readings require the assumption that the word order is odd, with the series of infinitives preceding the verbs on which they depend. Moreover, the Hebrew would be odd even if *lōʾ rāʾāh* preceded, since *rāʾāh* is not normally followed by an infinitive with *l.* Actually, it occurs in no case that I could discover; Budde (1898) makes the same observation. Hence it seems preferable to explain the infinitives as dependent on the parallel verbs in the preceding verse (v 33: *lōʾ ʿinnāh . . . wayyaggeh*). *ʾᵃdōnāy lōʾ rāʾāh* is then understood to be a circumstantial clause; cf. GKC, para. 156, d–g. On the meaning of the verse, see the COMMENT below. In any explanation, it remains a bit odd that names of God are used in the infinitive phrases of 35 and 36 instead of pronouns, as here in 34 ("under foot," literally, "under his feet"), but one may compare similar phenomena in 2:20, 22 and especially v 66 below: "May you (Yahweh is being addressed) pursue them in anger and wipe them out from under the LORD's

heaven!" Compare also, e.g., Amos 4:11: "I (Yahweh) overthrew some of you as when God overthrew Sodom and Gomorrah."

37. Since in this and the following verse it is obvious that the poet means to assert positively that God does command both good and bad, one must look on the *lōʾ* in each line as either (a) a negative, "not," and read the lines as rhetorical questions; or (b) asseverative or an emphatic *lamed*. This explanation is preferred by McDaniel (1968b: 206–8), where a bibliography on the emphatic *lamed* is given. The latter alternative has been adopted here, but the difference in sense is slight, whichever is chosen.

39. The MT has often been regarded as corrupt, but it seems defensible (Meek 1956, Weiser 1962, Kraus 1968, and Albrektson 1963 retain it), though the Hebrew is rather odd. A literal rendering would be "Why should a living man *(ʾādām ḥāy)* complain, a man *(geber)* over his sins." The phrase *ʾādām ḥāy* may be intended to suggest the idea "Where there's life, there's hope" (cf. the *keleb ḥay* of Eccl 9:4) and its converse in Israelite thought, that the dead have no hope. The parallelism seems to involve ellipsis from the second colon of the verb and interrogative, which must be supplied from the first colon.

40. *test. ḥāpaś* more frequently means "search for," but the idea here is not of trying to find the right path, but of examination of one's conduct; the parallel verb *ḥāqar* is often used so, and *ḥāpaś* has the sense "test" also in Prov 20:27.

41. *ʾel* is used for *ʿal*, as often. The sense is "with, along with," and it may deserve notice that this use of *ʿal* is especially common in prescriptions for sacrifice: X is to be sacrificed with *(ʿal)* Y; see BDB, s.v. *ʿal* 4c.

42. The close quote after v 41 and the opening quote at the beginning of v 42 are used here to mark a change in speakers; see the COMMENT below.

43. *You have enveloped.* The verb *sakkōtāh* is probably not reflexive, since elsewhere the *qal* is always transitive. Hence not "you covered yourself," but "you covered us," the object-pronoun on *wattirdᵉpēnū* serving for both verbs; cf. vv 2, 5, and 66 for similar shared objects. Note also that there is no objection to interpreting this first *sakkōtāh* (here) as a bit different in its syntactic function from the identical form in the next line; cf. the successive occurrences of *pᵉnē* in 4:16a and 16b.

51. *The affliction done to me . . . eyes.* The MT is corrupt and yields no acceptable sense, as recognized by most. Very literally rendered, the MT is "My eye has done to my soul from (or, more than) all the daughters of my people." Read perhaps *'ōnī 'ōlal l<sup>e</sup>napšī m<sup>e</sup>kall<eh> b<sup>e</sup>nōt 'ēnay.* For another case in which *'ōnī* has been confused with *'ēnī*, see 2 Sam 16:12. On *b<sup>e</sup>nōt 'ēnay*, cf. Lam 2:18, *bat 'ayin*. To the whole verse compare Ps 69:4 [ = 3E]: "I am worn out from calling, my throat is parched, my eyes are consumed *(kālū 'ēnay)."*

56. *Hear. šāmā'tā* is interpreted here as a precative perfect; see the NOTE on 1:21. In 55–66 these perfects are interspersed with imperative or other volitive forms, and note also the confirmation of this interpretation from Ps 130:1, a closely parallel passage: "From the depths I call you" *(q<sup>e</sup>rā'tīkā)* parallels v 55: "Out of the lowest pit, O LORD, I call *(qārā'tī)* your name"; and Ps 130:2, "Lord hear *(šim'āh*, an imperative) my voice" parallels v 56 *qōlī šāmā'tā* (perfect), which must then be "Hear my voice." Also interpreted as precative perfects in this passage are v 57, *qārabtā* and *'āmartā;* v 58, *rabtā* and *gā'altā;* v 59, *rā'ītāh;* v 60, *rā'ītāh;* and v 61, *šāma'tā.*

The latter part of v 56 is difficult grammatically and metrically (it is hard to find satisfactory division into two parts), but for lack of convincing improvement the MT has been retained and translated rather literally. The only change is from *l<sup>e</sup>šaw'ātī* ('to my cry') to *līšū'ātī* ('for my salvation, to save me'). The latter reading is supported by the LXX, Symmachus, and perhaps Syriac, and fits better with *l<sup>e</sup>rawḥātī* ('for my relief, to relieve me'). *l<sup>e</sup>rawḥātī* is odd after "Do not close your ears," where we expect as object (following *l*) either a person or a word meaning "cry, voice" or the like. Yet its aptness in this context is suggested by *qrw lh b'q' w'nn brwḥ' ln,* "they called on him (cf. v 55) in distress and he answered them with relief for them." These lines, from a Palmyrene Aramaic inscription (published by Dja'far al-Hassani and Jean Starcky, "Autels Palmyréniens découverts près de la source Efca," *Annales archéologiques de la Syrie* 3 [1953]: 160–63), are paralleled in another Palmyrene inscription published by Jean-Baptiste Chabot (*Corpus inscriptionum semiticarum,* pt. 2, vol. 3.1 [Paris, 1926], no. 4100). Chabot called attention to the biblical parallel in Ps 118:5, especially close when the Syriac and Targum of the verse are considered. These parallels (and, more remotely, Pss 18:20 [ = 19E];

31:9 [ = 8E]) caution against deletion of *l*e*rawḥātī*. Some (e.g., Rudolph 1962) have deleted *l*e*šawʿātti*, and indeed it looks suspiciously like a double reading; but deletion would leave a very short colon.

63. *in everything they do.* Literally, "(in) their sitting down and rising up." The combination of "sit" and "rise" is a familiar meristic idiom in Hebrew for the whole round of a person's daily activities; cf., e.g., Deut 6:7. The suffix -*ām* on each of the nouns is here construed as the possessive suffix "their." McDaniel (1968b: 204–5) takes it as an adverbial suffix (cf. the first NOTE on 2:18), and reinterprets other elements in the verse as well. But one may question whether sufficient evidence has up to now been advanced for free use of adverbial -*ām*, apart from the few stereotyped adverbs in which it has long been recognized. In other respects also, the MT seems defensible as it stands, despite unusual word order.

65. *anguish of heart.* Heb *m*e*ginnat lēb* is of uncertain meaning. This rendering, which is also that of *JPS*, at least fits the context. The *RSV*'s "dullness of heart" (*NRSV* "anguish of heart") is preferred by many commentators, who associate the word with a root *gnn* 'cover', but this reading seems too weak for the context. Rudolph (1962) and Kraus (1968) suggest "delusion, confusion," which also fits reasonably well, but is scarcely established by the etymology supplied (Ar *jinn, majnūn*).

66. *pursue them.* The object "them" is supplied from the following verb ("and wipe them out"). G. R. Driver was the first to point out that in cases of parallel words only one needs an explicit pronominal suffix in Hebrew poetic style; he cited this passage as an example (see "Hebrew Studies," *Journal of the Royal Asiatic Society*" [1948]: 164–65). Compare now Dahood, *Psalms III, 101–50*, AB 17C (Garden City, NY, 1970), 431–32.

# COMMENT

Chapter 3 stands apart from the other chapters of the book in both form and content. Formally, it is an alphabetic acrostic poem, like 1, 2, and 4; and, as in 1 and 2, the stanzas each have three lines. The acrostic is of a more demanding type, however, since the initial word of each of the three lines is made to fit the acrostic pattern. Thus there are three *aleph* lines, three *beth* lines, and so on. This elaborateness is surpassed only in Ps 119. In addition, the author is fond of repeating the initial word or particle, or employing words of the same grammatical form in initial position (see the INTRODUCTION). A counterrhythm to the strict march of the acrostic pattern is provided by the sequence of thought, for very often breaks in the thought occur within the stanzas; and, correspondingly, ideas are conjoined across the stanzas as divided by the acrostic. Thus in sense v 3 goes with v 4 (see below), 6 with 7, 12 with 13, 18 with 19–20, 21 with 22ff., 42 with 43–47, 48 with 49–51, and 60 with 61–63.

In content chapter 3 differs from the others in that there is very little specific reference to the fall of Jerusalem or the sufferings that followed. The poem begins, "I am the man who has seen hardship," and it continues for a long time to speak of how this man has suffered. Thus one of the major questions that arises is: How is this chapter connected with the rest of the book? Another is: Who is this man? These questions are complicated by the presence of other voices within the poem: "we" is used in v 40–47, and though the first-person singular pronoun "I" returns at vv 48–51 and 52–66, one is led to ask whether this "I" is the same as the one who speaks in the first part of the poem.

The tradition that Jeremiah was the author of Lamentations provided a ready-made answer for the major questions posed by the chapter: Jeremiah is the man, and he speaks of his own sufferings. The other voices that are heard in the poem are readily explained as responding to his words. When one abandons the idea of authorship by Jeremiah, however, some other explanation must be found for the "man" of v 1. Various approaches to an answer are summarized below; the reader should keep in mind that for all the variety of opinion represented there are often considerable areas of agreement between one scholar and another—the various approaches are not always mutually exclusive alternatives.

A favorite line of interpretation has been to see the "I" who speaks in the poem as collective. This view has been held, for example, by R. Smend, Ehrlich (1914), Eissfeldt (*Einleitung in das Alte Testament* [Tübingen, 1964], pp. 680–81), Gottwald (1962), and Albrektson (1963). It is Zion who speaks, Zion represented as an individual, as in chapters 1 and 2. Also Giuseppe Ricciotti, who holds the opinion that Jeremiah wrote the book, comes close to this

collective view because he sees Jeremiah in his suffering as identified with Jerusalem in a particularly intimate way (1924: 78, note
on v 1). This interpretation has the advantage of tying chapter 3
closely to the rest of the book, and also of accounting for the
intrusion of "we" passages toward the end of the poem—the "I"
and "we" are in a sense identical, since the community is speaking
throughout. Yet this view, especially for vv 1–36, encounters serious
difficulties. Zion is a woman, a mother, in the other poems, whereas
the speaker in chapter 3 is unmistakably male, a *geber*. The contrast
is especially sharp because v 1, "I am the man," immediately follows the last verses of chapter 2, with their picture of the bereaved
mother Zion. Furthermore, the speaker in 3 is explicitly set apart
from "my people" (*'ammī*, 14)—a point that evidently bothered
ancient adherents to the collective theory as well, since the reading
is changed to "peoples" (*'ammīm*) in the Syriac, some Greek manuscripts, and also in a Sebir having reference to the Masoretic Text,
and in some Hebrew manuscripts. In my view, a collective theory is
easier to maintain for the "I" of vv 52–66 than for the first part of
the poem, but though such a view is of considerable value in understanding the poem, it falls short of doing justice to everything in
the chapter.

At the opposite end of the spectrum, there are others who have
read this chapter as a poem about an individual; for example, Bernhard Stade (*Geschichte Israels*, vol. 1 [Berlin, 1887], 701 n. 1) and
Budde in his commentary (1898). In the view of these scholars, the
chapter has little to do with the rest of the book, and in fact was
written much later. It is not concerned with the fall of Jerusalem in
587 B.C. at all. This view has the merit of acknowledging that much
of the poem is about an individual's troubles, but it cannot account
convincingly for the presence of the "we" passages, with their references to a more than personal disaster. Moreover it seems very
superficial if, having established that the chapter deals with an
individual, one concludes at once that this must separate it drasti-
cally from the rest of the book. At least one ought to look for ways
in which this poem—which is, if only physically and formally, central to the book—is integrated with it in thought.

Some have identified the "man" of the poem with a specific
historic individual. Norman W. Porteous has argued, rather briefly,
that the "man" must be King Jehoiachin (1961: 244–45). He seems

not to have been followed by others in this identification, and indeed there is no specific evidence in favor of it. Rudolph (1962), like some others before him—for example, Stade, Löhr, and Budde—identifies the "man" as the prophet Jeremiah—not that Jeremiah wrote the book, or this poem, but that the anonymous author makes Jeremiah appear so as to provide his people with an example of how faith in God triumphs over suffering. Meek also entertains this idea (1956), but he does not develop it at length. Rudolph's exegesis is illuminating, both in many individual details and in its broad explanation of the meaning of chapter 3 within the book; yet on this one point, the identification of the sufferer with Jeremiah, it is unconvincing. The description of the man's sufferings, as will be shown in detail below, is cast almost exclusively in traditional figurative language, for which parallels can easily be found in the psalms of lament or in other writings of similar theme, notably Job. To say that this language is traditional is not to say that it is flat or insincere; it seems to me illuminating to compare the intensely felt words of "La pietà," of Giuseppe Ungaretti (1928), which begins "I am a wounded man" (translated in *The Penguin Book of Italian Verse*, ed. G. R. Kay [Baltimore, 1958]). But there is nothing in the chapter that makes it necessary to think that Jeremiah, or for that matter any of the writer's contemporaries, is the one who speaks.

The view adopted here is that the sufferer of chapter 3 is indeed an individual, not a collective figure like the Zion of chapters 1 and 2. This individual is, however, not a specific historical figure, but rather anyone who has suffered greatly. He is an "Everyman," a figure who represents what any man may feel when it seems that God is against him. Through this representative sufferer the poet points the way to the nation, as he shows the man who has been through trouble moving into, then out of, near despair to patient faith and penitence, thus becoming a model for the nation. This is the high point of the book, central to it in more than an external or formal way.

Such a line of interpretation has been taken, in major respects, by Keil (1872) and Oettli (1889) in the last century, and by others since, most recently Kraus (1968). Rudolph's view is similar in essentials, except that he also identifies the "man" as Jeremiah, as explained above. In his commentary (1866: 324), Ewald expressed the sense of the poem with particular clarity:

> Then, suddenly, in the third place, an individual man appears! After all, an individual is able really to lament most deeply what he has experienced personally. The result is an expression of despair—the third, but this is the deepest. However, it is also easier for an individual to engage in deep private contemplation of the eternal relation of God to man, and thus come to a proper recognition of his own sins and the necessity of repentance, and thereby to believing prayer. Who is this individual who thus laments, reflects, and prays!—whose "I" unnoticed but at exactly the right point changes to "We"? O man, he is the image of your own self! Everyone should speak and think as he does. And so it comes about, unexpectedly, that just through this discourse which is most difficult at its beginning, for the first time pain is transformed into true prayer.

I agree with Kraus, however, that the "I" who speaks at the end (vv 52–66) is not identical with the "I" of the beginning; at any rate, because of the preceding collective prayer in vv 42–51, the reader is led to think that the speaker of the closing verses is praying on behalf of, or is representing, the people. The following outline summarizes the progress of thought in this rather difficult poem; details are discussed in the comments that follow.

A.  An individual sufferer achieves patient faith and penitence, vv 1–39

  1.  The sufferings a man went through, 1–16

  2.  They lead him to despair, 17–20

  3.  But he achieves hope by recalling the mercy of God, 21–39

    a.  God's mercy is abiding, 21–25

    b.  Even suffering must be good, 26–30

    c.  Because God is good and just, 31–39

B. Transition: the sufferer calls on his people to return to God, vv 40–41

C. A common prayer of lamentation and supplication, vv 42–66

    1. The people speak: We have sinned and are suffering for it, 42–47

    2. The poet's grief over his people's ruin—if only Yahweh would see! 48–51

    3. An appeal for Yahweh to help, spoken by an individual, 52–66

At the beginning the sufferer makes a general statement—I have been through trouble—then he proceeds through the whole first section of the chapter (1b–16) to describe his suffering in a series of more or less isolated pictures. Most of the language is figurative rather than literal. Most of the language is also traditional, since similar things are said in psalms of lament, in Job, and elsewhere. The language and thought are for the most part clear and readily understandable without further explanation, and for this reason the specific comments that follow are mostly intended to point out parallels in other literature, and to indicate where possible the associations that link individual images. This emphasis on a rather full listing of parallels for each of the verses is also intended to substantiate the assertion made above, namely, that the "man" cannot be identified with any specific individual, as some commentators have proposed. Through v 9, the dominant theme might be called a reversal of the Twenty-third Psalm: the Lord is a shepherd who misleads, a ruler who oppresses and imprisons. Or one might call it the opposite of the picture of salvation found in the Exodus and wilderness traditions and in Second Isaiah; the vocabulary and imagery here are the same at numerous points, but turned to depict judgment, not grace.

"The rod of his anger" (cf. Prov 22:8 and Isa 10:5) is figurative for divine punishment, as frequently in the Old Testament, for instance, 2 Sam 7:14; Ps 89:33 [ = 32E]; Job 9:34; 21:9. The rod was used for chastising children, and was also carried by rulers as a symbol of their exercise of force. Shepherds also carried staves, only one of the metaphoric links between pastoral life and political life. Hence it is not inconceivable that this is the link between the "rod (*šēbeṭ*)" of v 1 and the "leading" of v 2. Often God's leading or directing a person, or Israel (Hebrew words used are *nāhag*, *hōlīk*, *hidrīk*, *nāḥāh*, *naḥḥēl*) is explicitly compared to the leading of a flock or herd (Pss 77:21 [ = 20E]; 78:52–53; 80:2 [ = 1E]; Isa 40:11; 63:13–14; etc.). In an overwhelming majority of cases the picture of divine leading is one of salvation. It is frequently part of the description of God's care for Israel in the wilderness, in the days of Moses (Exod 15:13; Pss 77:21 [ = 20E]; 78:52–53) and in the new exodus out of captivity (Isa 63:13–14; 49:10; cf. Isa 40:11). For that reason the present verse is especially bold, and the sentence structure, with its suspenseful pause after the verbs, underscores the drastic reversal: "He led and guided me—into darkness and gloom." (Compare Amos 5:18.)

Deliverance from darkness is also salvation imagery, associated especially often with the new exodus. While light stands for all that is positive and good, it specifically connotes freedom in some cases, just as darkness is figurative for imprisonment (cf. Isa 42:6–7, 16; 49:9; 58:9–12; Pss 43:3; 107:10–16). This line, then, with its suggestion of a change from freedom to imprisonment, anticipates much in the following lines, especially vv 6 and 7. (On walking in darkness, v 2, cf. also Isa 50:10; Ps 82:5; Eccl 2:14.) The specific phrase "turned his hand against (*yahᵃpōk yādō*)," v 3, is not otherwise used of divine activity toward men, but it is obviously intended to express hostile action. By itself, the "hand" of God frequently is a name for some calamity, especially sickness; cf. Job 19:21; 1 Sam 5:6; etc., and the study by J. J. Roberts of the expression "hand of God" in Israelite and other ancient literature, *VT* 21 (1971): 244–51. This reference to God's hand thus leads naturally into v 4, with its reference to the flesh, skin, and bones of the sufferer. This is a recurrent motif in psalms of lament. Especially close is Ps 38:3–4 [ = 2–3E]: "For your arrows have sunk into me (cf. vv 12–13, below), and your hand has come down on me. There is no soundness in my flesh because of your indignation; there is no health in my bones because of my sin." Other close parallels, in vocabulary and thought, are Isa 38:13; Ps 32:3–4.

"Besieged (*bānāh ʿālay*)" in v 5 seems to involve comparison of the speaker to a city encircled by enemies; cf. Deut 20:20; 2 Kgs 25:1; Eccl 9:14. "Encircled (*hiqqīp ʿal*)" is used of towns and also, in laments, of people beset by enemies (Pss 17:9; 22:17 [ = 16E]) or by God's wrath and terrors (Ps 88:18 [= 17E]). The last passage cited is similar to the present verse in that abstractions (here: penury and hardship) are named as the besiegers.

As stated above, "he made me sit in the dark" is a semifigurative expression for "He put me in prison" (Ps 107:10–16; Isa 42:6–7; 49:9; cf. also Pss 88:7 [= 6E]; 143:3; Mic 7:8). The prison picture is carried through into the next line and made more explicit there (v 7). At the same time, the picture of sitting or dwelling in darkness suggests the realm of the dead—indeed, "the Dark" is a poetic term for Sheol; see Ps 88:13 [= 12E]; Job 10:21–22; 17:13; 18:18; Eccl 6:4; 11:8. Hence the comparison follows: "like those long dead," a simile that recurs in Pss 31:13 [= 12E]; 88:5–7 [= 4–6E]; Isa 59:10 (in Ps 143:3 the wording is identical, but the text may have been influenced by v 6). The dead are forgotten and cut off from Yahweh's attention and intervention, a line of thought resumed in v 8.

The reference to being walled in and chained is not to be taken as an allusion to events in the life of Jeremiah, as Rudolph (1962) would have it, though the prophet did experience confinement in various ways (20:1–3; 37:21; 38:6–13; 40:1; cf. 29:26). In the first place, the surrounding lines are figurative for various sorts of distress, and one may question an exegesis that would single out just these as literally true. Second, this sort of image recurs in other poems. The closest parallels to the present text are Job 13:27 (repeated in 33:11): "You put my feet in the stocks, and watch over my paths." Note also Ps 88:9 [= 8E]: "I am imprisoned, and cannot escape." Compare also Pss 105:18; 107:10–16; 116:16; Isa 28:22, all of which mention the bonds of prisoners; and Ps 142:8 [= 7E].

Even though this man of sorrows calls to God, God has shut out his prayer (v 8). Once again, this is a stock theme of laments. It occurs again in v 44, and in closely parallel form at Hab 1:2 and Job 19:7; 30:20. The most common expression used is that God "hides his face"; see Isa 59:2 and many other passages.

A new theme appears at v 9 (though there is a verbal link with 7; the initial word is gādar in both verses): God has "blocked up" and "made crooked" the sufferer's "path"—in nonfigurative language, God has frustrated his purposes and kept him from pursuing the kind of life he wanted. Job 3:23 and Hos 2:8 [= 6E] also speak of God's blocking up a person's path, and Ps 146:9 speaks of God's twisting the way of the wicked (cf. v 11 below and, for a verbal parallel, Jer 3:21). Just why "cut stones" (*gāzīt*) should be mentioned specifically is uncertain, but the idea may be that this material, used only in the finest, most substantial buildings in ancient Israel, is specified in order to indicate that God has walled the man in as solidly as possible. Weiser (1962) paraphrases by saying that the man finds himself in a cul-de-sac no matter where he turns. The path motif may have provided the transition to the picture of God as a bear and lion, the idea being that these predators lie in wait beside a man's path.

The bear and the lion, frequently mentioned together as the most dangerous of all beasts, are figurative for a man's enemies also, for example, in Pss 22:14 [ = 13E] and 10:9 (the latter passage is close to the present verse in that the lion is said to lie in wait for its prey). Occasionally God in his anger is compared to a bear or lion; cf. Isa 38:13 and especially Hos 13:8, which is very similar to the present passage.

The vivid picture of God deliberately setting up a helpless man as his target recurs in Job 16:12–13; cf. Job 6:4; Ps 38:3 [ = 2E]; Lam 2:4. The main point of the picture is simply that God assails a man, but it is also possible that the poet meant to suggest that God afflicts man with sickness, since "arrows" are rather often figurative for disease: cf., e.g., Job 34:6; Ps 91:5, and the memorable scene at the beginning of the *Iliad*, in which the archer Apollo shoots shafts of pestilence into the Greek camp. These verses (12–13) are linked to the foregoing not by sense but by sound: 11 begins *dᵉrākay* and 12, *dārak*.

The cruel laughter of the man's own people (see the NOTE) is part of what he had to endure. This is mentioned again in v 63; for other parallels see the COMMENT on 1:7. The specific reference to taunting songs recurs at v 63 and in Job 30:9. Reference to having to drink bitter things (v 15) was also apparently a commonplace image for suffering; cf. v 19 and Jer 9:14 [ = 15E]; Job 9:18.

Since both verbs used in v 16 are very rare and of somewhat uncertain meaning, it is not clear exactly what picture is intended. It seems likely that approximately the same situation is depicted in both parts of the line. If so, there are many parallels in laments to "trampling in the dirt," for example, Ps 7:6 [ = 5E], and "he ground my teeth in the gravel" may be an equivalent for the more common "lick the dust," cf. Ps 72:9; Mic 7:17; also Ps 102:10 [ = 9E].

As stated above, then, the poet has to this point presented the plaint of a sufferer in pictures that are conventional and typical rather than sharply individual. We are thus prevented from identifying the speaker with any specific man, and are compelled to believe that the writer intended something other than a portrait of a contemporary: he meant to show human suffering as it is commonly and generally felt by men in dark times, when God appears as an enemy. For a time he deliberately draws attention away from the particular events of 587 B.C., as if to say: Look—this is what any man may go through.

The following passage (vv 17–21) is transitional. Now the man tells of his inner reaction to all his suffering: he is led to despair, and then to hope. The sentence with which he sums up the situation: "I thought, 'My lasting hope in the LORD has perished,' " is already a hint that a turning point is coming, because this sort of direct speech, beginning "I thought (said) . . ." is occasionally used in laments at just such points. Thus in Jonah 2:5 [ = 4E]: "So I said, 'I have been driven from your sight.' Yet I will continue to look to your holy temple." Very similar are Pss 31:23 [ = 22E]; 94:18; 139:11; cf. also Isa 6:5; 38:11; 49:4.

Depending on which translation is adopted for vv 19–20 (see the NOTES), the expression of a hopeful attitude either follows at once, at v 19, or, as translated here, begins at v 21, after an amplified description of the man's inner despondency (vv 19–20). The one cause for hope is the mercy of Yahweh (ḥesed 'steadfast love' or 'loyal love'). This is not a passing phase in God, but an enduring part of his nature, always being renewed toward mankind, and an ancient part of Israel's faith. Quite appropriately, Weiser (1962) compares God's description of his nature (Exod 34:6–7), in the course of his appearance to Moses on Sinai: "Yahweh, a god merciful and gracious, patient, and abounding in mercy and faithfulness." On the basis of this enduring mercy the speaker asserts that even in trials Yahweh is "his share." The expression arises in the traditions about the division of the Promised Land. All Israelites received allotments, but not the priests, for God said to Aaron (Num 18:20): "I am your portion." At the most literal level this meant that the priests were to live from offerings, but the expression came to be a way of asserting that when every other support for life failed, Yahweh remained: "My flesh and my heart may fail, but God is . . . my portion forever" (Ps 73:26 RSV). Not God's love, but his anger is a passing phase, and thus even of suffering the first word of faith can be "Good"; the poet puts this "good" (Heb *tōb*) at the beginning of the next three lines (vv 25–27). It is good to wait in hope for Yahweh's mercy to show itself. It is good for a man if he has to carry the yoke of trials (cf. 1:14). "In his youth" (or "from his youth," as the phrase might also be rendered) seems to stress that suffering has educational value, just as, in the Israelite view, corporal punishment was good for the young (Prov 13:24; 22:15; 23:13–14; 29:15). The phrase "in his youth" is thus not to be pressed for biographical information about the speaker; it is, as Albrektson (1963) notes, a general, almost proverbial observation.

When suffering comes, a man should be passive and utterly abase himself before God. To "put the mouth in the dirt" was an age-old act of obeisance and of humiliation before a superior among the peoples of the ancient Near East (cf. Mic 7:17; Ps 72:9). It is implied that this prostration is before Yahweh, hence one ought probably to understand the expression "the one who strikes him" in v 30 as a reference to Yahweh instead of to a human. Although Luther in translating this passage deliberately omitted the "maybe" from "maybe there is hope" as too fainted-hearted for properly robust faith, this phrase is not so much an expression of wavering faith as a recognition that God is sovereign and free; it is the voice of piety, not of doubt. Ancient Israelites rather often said "maybe" about the possibility that Yahweh would act favorably in a particular case (Exod 32:30; Num 23:3, 27; Josh 14:12; etc.); or for similar reason they say "Who knows?" (2 Sam 12:22; Joel 2:14; Jonah 3:9).

The degree of humility required of man is deliberately stated in extreme terms, so as to prepare for the forceful statement—a threefold "because"—of the reasons for patient trust. God does not cast a person off forever, and though he inflicts pain it is followed by compassion. Afflicting people is not deliberate on his part; literally translated, the text says (v 33) that it is not "from his heart."

This passage is a kind of resolution in advance of the paradox that is stated in vv 37–38: both good and bad happen by command of God. While this is true, as it must be since God is the creator who "spoke and it was done" (v 37; cf. Num 23:19; Ps 33:9), yet suffering, pain, and evil are not his final intention. He does not act like a tyrant, mistreating prisoners and denying men justice. The lines that make this assertion (34–36; see the NOTES) seem to draw on traditional descriptions of unjust rule. The tyrant king of Babylon "did not let his prisoners go home" (Isa 14:17; text somewhat uncertain). Yahweh's concern for the imprisoned, in contrast, is frequently mentioned: for example, Pss 68:7 [ = 6E]; 69:34 [ = 32E]; 107:10–16. "The prisoners of the earth" is probably a reference to prisoners in general (cf. $^{c a}n\bar{\imath}yy\bar{e}$ '$\bar{a}ye\d{s}$, Job 24:4) instead of to "the prisoners of the land (Judah)," which would be a reference to the captives in Babylon. There are many biblical references to perversion of justice by rulers, and associated with them one occasionally finds it stated that the wicked imagine that "Yahweh does not see" (Pss 64:6 [ = 5E]; 94:2–7; Ezek 8:12; 9:9; cf. Isa 47:10; Isa 29:15; Jer 12:4). This association may account for the presence here of the clauses "before the Most High" and "without the Lord seeing," which are slightly incongruous in a sentence describing the Lord; but the whole verse is syntactically difficult (see the NOTE) and the interpretation uncertain.

God is, after all, the creator (v 37), and though he brings about both good things and bad things (calamities, trouble, not moral evil; cf. Amos 3:6), this reference to his creative omnipotence is intended to be comforting, because the creator and what he has made cannot in the final analysis be evil. Hence the speaker turns to consider man's proper response, in a line that looks both forward and back. By repeating the "man" of v 1, it rounds off the poem and calls attention to the progress in thought to this point. We have come from a complaint beginning "I am the man," through submission, to the conclusion "Why should a man complain?" (v 39). A new note is added with the reference to "his punishment." Even though the sense of the Hebrew word, which in many contexts means "sins," here is more probably the less common sense, "what his sins have brought on him" (see BDB, s.v. $h\bar{e}\d{t}$, no. 3; cf. Ps 38:4 [ = 3E]; Zech 14:19), this is the first time it is implied in the poem that the man's troubles have been due to his own sins —he is being punished—and that he should call into question not the goodness of God but his own goodness. Thus the line leads into the ensuing call for repentance.

The brief summons to repentance calls for three things: self-examination, repentance—the usual term "return" is employed—and sincerity. Sincerity is demanded in the phrase "let us lift our heart along with our hands" (v 41), which emphasizes that the inner attitude must accompany the outward gesture. The intent is much like the familiar "Rend your heart and not your garments" of Joel 2:13.

Rather unobtrusively the plural of the exhortation ("Let us") is carried over into the prayer that follows: "We have rebelled." The result, however, is a major shift in point of view. Suddenly the voice of the whole people is heard, and the concern is once again that of the previous chapters, the ruin of the nation. It seems best to regard all of vv 42–66 as belonging to this collective prayer, in spite of the obviously disparate elements. The prayer is not entirely made up of explicit petitions for help, since there is a good deal that describes distress, but this is a normal feature of collective laments, a good example being chapter 5 of this book. Note that in spite of superficial resemblance to lines in the complaint that began the present chapter, this passage is at a fundamentally different stage. There the idea was to depict a man's troubles so as to show his inner progress from despair to hope, whereas here suffering is described in order to awaken Yahweh's pity—all is turned toward God. The "we" that begins the prayer is maintained only as far as v 47. Thereafter the poet speaks, in the first-person singular, as one observing the ruin of his people (vv 48–51). This point of view is abandoned in turn in favor of a subjective description of the troubles and a petition, but this time not in the first-person plural ("we"), rather in the singular ("I"). This is a return to the style of the first part of the chapter, but the introduction of the whole people in the preceding section brings the collective sense much more strongly to the fore than was true in the earlier section; hence one may think of this "I" passage as a continuation and completion of the collective prayer. It may appear inconsistent to make a distinction between the "I" of the end and the "I" of the beginning of the poem, but it seems justified when one recalls that someone reading the poem, or a worshiper hearing it in a service, experiences the poem serially, starting at the beginning, and is not likely to have the end in mind at the start.

The first line of the prayer (v 42) states the basic situation: we have rebelled, and you have not forgiven, as is evident from what has happened and is still happening to us. You have slain us unsparingly (cf. 2:21) and then shut out our prayers for help (v 44; for parallels see v 8 above). The reference to God's wrapping himself in "cloud *('ānān)*" may be merely a picturesque metaphor, but more likely this is a reference to a permanent part of Yahweh's nature, as Israel conceived it: he is enveloped by a radiant *'ānān,* through which he reveals himself, by which he overwhelms enemies, and in which he may hide himself, as here. Similar conceptions of deities were held in Mesopotamia and Canaan (cf. George Mendenhall, "The Mask of Yahweh," in *The Tenth Generation* [Baltimore and London, 1973], 32–66). Reference to Israel's enemies at the end of the stanza (v 45) leads into the next: "All our enemies open their mouths wide at us." (For this stock motif see the COMMENT on 2:15.) The next line is a variant on stock expressions that must have been proverbial in ancient Israel, to judge from their recurrence in the Old Testament (Isa 24:17–18; Jer 48:43–44) and the alliteration and assonance of the Hebrew (*paḥad wāpaḥat . . . haššē't wehaššāber;* the translation "panic and pit, wreck and ruin" attempts to suggest the effect). Such assonance is a characteristic of pairs of words in certain Hebrew idioms, much like the English "house and home."

The point of view changes, and for a brief space the poet speaks of his grief at the ruin of his people (vv 48–51). He will weep unceasingly (cf. 1:16; 2:18; Ps 119:136) until Yahweh looks down in pity. Although the connection to the rest of the prayer is loose, this indirect appeal does supply a link to the context.

The lament and prayer resume at v 52 except that, as stated, the prayer is cast in the singular. The theme of suffering is briefly touched on. The themes are traditional: he is being hunted like a bird (cf., e.g., Pss 11:1; 124:7; 140:6 [ = 5E]; Jer 16:16; and the COMMENT on 1:13), and has been thrown into a pit where—a motif that seems to be unparalleled—they throw stones down at him. The infernal connotations of the word "pit" are taken up in the next line, when it is said that waters came up over his head. These are the waters of Sheol, a traditional image for really desperate trouble; cf. Jonah 2:6–7 [ = 5–6E]; 2 Sam 22:5–6 = Pss 18:5–6 [ = 4–5E]; 69:2–3, 15–16 [ = 1–2, 14–15E]. In the first part of the chapter, Yahweh himself was the enemy, but now there is reference to "Those who are my enemies for no reason." This echoes "our enemies" in v 46, and touches a theme that dominates the remainder of the chapter: Yahweh is to help against the enemies. If it is correct to understand the "I" in this part of the poem as collective, then the enemies are foreign: Babylon and Edom (cf. 4:21–22).

The reference to the pit and to the infernal waters sets the stage for the *De profundis* that follows, in which even the language is strikingly similar to that of the familiar psalm (cf. vv 55–56 and Ps 130:1–2; see the NOTE). In every way at his command the speaker begs Yahweh to listen, observe, help, and take up his cause against his enemies, who constantly plot against him, deny him his rights, and mock him. All that is asked is that they be treated as they have treated their fellow man. This is the longest exposition of such an idea in Lamentations; shorter presentations of it occur at 1:21–22 and 4:21–22. That God should deal out retribution to Israel's enemies, or torment to a man's tormentors, is a typical Old Testament theme. Even when Israel was conscious of her own rebellion against God, as in this poem (vv 39–42), and acknowledged the justice of such punishment as was meted out to her, this guilt never meant to her that her enemies were justified in the atrocities they committed. On the contrary, belief in divine justice meant that Yahweh should deal just as strictly with the nations as he did with Israel.

## IV
## The Limit of Suffering
## (4:1–22)

| | | |
|---|---|---|
| *aleph* | 4:1 | How gold is despised!   Good gold is hated! Jewels are scattered about   at every street corner! |
| *beth* | 2 | The people of Zion, so precious,   worth their weight in finegold, Are now treated like cheap crockery,   the work of the potter. |
| *gimel* | 3 | Even a jackal will offer her teats   and suckle her cubs, But my people is truly cruel,   like the ostriches in the desert. |
| *daleth* | 4 | The tongue of the suckling child, from thirst,   sticks to its palate. Young children ask for bread;   no one gives it to them. |
| *he* | 5 | Those who once fed on delicacies   are destitute in the streets; Those brought up in scarlet clothing   pick through garbage. |
| *waw* | 6 | So the wickedness of my people was greater   than the sin of Sodom, Which was overthrown in a moment,   without a hand laid on it. |
| *zayin* | 7 | Her Nazirites were whiter than snow,   lighter than milk. Their bodies were more ruddy than corals,   their beards were like dark stone. |
| *heth* | 8 | Now they look blacker than soot;   they are not recognized in the street. Their skin has shrunk over their bones,   has become dry as wood. |
| *teth* | 9 | Those killed by the sword were more fortunate   than those killed by famine; |

135

Those who perished of wounds,    than those who lacked the fruits of the field.

*yod*    10 With their own hands kindly women    cooked their children.
That was the food they had,    when my people was ruined.

*kaph*    11 The Lord gave full vent to his rage,    he poured out his hot anger,
And he started a fire in Zion    that burned its foundations.

*lamed*    12 The kings of the earth could not believe,    nor could anyone living on the earth,
That enemies and foes would pass    through the gates of Jerusalem.

*mem*    13 On account of the sins of her prophets,    the iniquities of her priests,
Who shed within her    the blood of the innocent,

*nun*    14 They wandered blind in the streets,    defiled with blood;
By exertion they are spent and exhausted;    their clothing is tattered.

*samekh*    15 "Get away! Unclean!" they call to them.    "Get away! Don't touch!"
"For they have gone away and must wander," they say.    "They shall no longer abide among the nations."

*pe*    16 The splendor of the Lord destroyed them.    He stopped looking after them.
He did not respect the priests,    or spare the elders.

*ayin*    17 We kept awake and wore out our eyes    looking for help—in vain.
On our lookout we kept watch    for a nation that does not save.

*sade*    18 They hunted our steps    so we could not walk in our streets.
Our end drew near, our time was up,    and our end came.

*qof*  19 Our pursuers were swifter   than eagles in the sky.

They were hot after us in the mountains;   they lay in ambush for us in the desert.

*resh*  20 The breath of our nostrils, the anointed of the Lord,   was caught in their traps,

The one of whom we said,   "In his shadow we will live among the nations."

*sin*  21 Rejoice and be glad, O Edom,   you who dwell in the land of Uz,

The cup will come round to you also,   and you will get drunk and strip naked.

*taw*  22 Your punishment is complete, O Zion!   He will not exile you again.

May he punish your iniquity, O Edom!   May he lay bare your sins!

# NOTES

**4 1.** *is despised . . . is hated!* The translation is based on emending the MT's *yūʿam* to *yūʿab*, and repointing *yišneʾ* to *yiśśāneʾ* (so already Ehrlich 1914; Ehrlich, however, emends the first verb to *yizzāʿēm* 'is cursed'). Ordinarily the text has been rendered "How the gold has grown dim; how the pure gold has changed!" following the ancient versions; but though linguistically possible this translation does not yield satisfactory sense. For one thing, gold does not tarnish or grow dark in any striking way, one of its principal qualities being that it stays bright. Figurative language involving gold in the OT never otherwise makes reference to the color or brightness of gold; the point of the comparison is always its value. For another, the first line of v 1 must fit the second, and v 2 as well, for the "gold" image is resumed there, and is explained as applying to the men of Zion. But with the stones of 1b and the men of v 2, the idea is that something happens to them from without, not that there is an internal change. As usually translated, the image in 1a is out of harmony with what follows. In favor of the conjecture proposed here, note the following. (a) The change from *yišneʾ* to *yiśśāneʾ* does not involve any change of consonants; in fact, it accounts

137

for the otherwise anomalous *aleph* of the MT. The *niphʿal* of *śānēʾ* occurs at Prov 14:20 (possibly also 14:17). (b) *śānēʾ* occurs as a parallel to, or in association with, *tōʿēbāh* 'abomination' or *tāʿēb* 'to abominate' in Prov 6:16; Ps 119:163; Amos 5:10; Deut 12:31. (c) The interchange of *mem* and *beth* is attested as a scribal error fairly commonly. On the derivation of *hōʿīb* see the NOTE at 2:1. (d) The translation yields a consistent image, the point throughout being that what is intrinsically precious is treated as worthless.

*Jewels.* *ʾabnē qōdeš*, if understood as "holy stones," is a puzzling phrase, especially since commentators are right in rejecting the idea that this could be a reference to the stones of the temple. Without emennding the text, J. A. Emerton (1967) explains *qōdeš* not as "holy" but as "jewel, ornament" on the basis of Aramaic, Arabic, and Akkadian cognates, and his suggestion has been adopted here. An early Aramaic occurrence of the word is in the Targum of Job from Qumran, where *qdš* translates Heb *nezem* (Job 42:11) 'ring (of gold)'; see J. P. M. van der Ploeg and A. S. van der Woude, *Le Targum de Job de la grotte XI de Qumrân* (Leiden, 1971), col. 38 line 8. On the possible Akkadian cognate see also K. Deller, "Die Briefe des Adad-šumu-uṣur," in *lišān mithurti*, ed. W. Röllig, Alter Orient und Altes Testament 1 (Kevelaer and Neukirchen-Vluyn, 1968), 53. Julius Wellhausen, *Skizzen und Vorarbeiten* vol. 5, 2d ed. (Berlin, 1893), 184, arrived at the sense "jewels" by taking "holy stones" as meaning "amulets." For comparison of a person to a jewel, cf. "The Babylonian Theodicy," lines 56–57: "O palm, tree of wealth, my precious brother / Endowed with all wisdom, jewel of gold." Cf. also Cart 5:11–15, and the imagery in the Sumerian "Message of Ludingira to His Mother"; see Jerrold S. Cooper, "New Cuneiform Parallels to the Song of Songs," *JBL* 90 (1971): 157–62.

*at every street corner.* The Hebrew literally means "at the head of all the streets"; cf. Isa 51:20; Lam 2:19d.

2. *worth their weight.* For this translation of the difficult *mᵉsullāʾīm*, cf. Job 28:16, 19.

3. *jackal.* In the Hebrew, literally "the jackals." The plural ending *-īn* instead of the usual *-īm* occurs here as also in 1:4. There is no need to see here the word *tannīn(īm)* 'sea-monster' or 'whale', as is done in the *New English Bible*, apparently based on G. R. Driver, "Mythical Monsters in the Old Testament," *Studi oriental-*

*istici in onore di G. Levi della Vida* vol. 1 (Rome, 1956), 246. Gr *drakontes* rests on a confusion.

*offer.* Heb *ḥālᵉṣū* 'draw out', probably transferred from human behavior instead of being characteristic of the animal.

*my people.* "Daughter of my people"; see the INTRODUCTION. Some emend to "daughters (plural) of my people," *bᵉnōt*, on the ground that the line applies only to the women, but that interpretation seems overly literal. Note, however, that it is unusual to find *bat ʿammī* first in a line.

*truly cruel.* Based on taking *l* in *lᵉʾakzār* as emphatic *lamed*, as first proposed by Israel Eitan, "Hebrew and Semitic Particles— Continued," *American Journal of Semitic Languages and Literatures* 45 (1928): 202 (cf. McDaniel 1968b: 206–8). 4Q179 II 4 reads *bt ʿmy ʾkzryh*. From this verse it seems that *ʾakzār*, like the closely related *ʾakzārī* (see Jer 50:42 and Prov 12:10), is indeclinable in Biblical Hebrew.

*ostriches.* Reading *kayᵉʿēnīm* with the *qere* and elsewhere.

5. *pick through garbage.* Literally, "have embraced refuse heaps."

6. The verse begins with the *waw*-consecutive; see the NOTE on 1:6.

*wickedness.* Here Heb *ʿāwōn* could also be translated "punishment," a sense well attested elsewhere, e.g., v 22 of this chapter; consequently, one could translate "the punishment" or the like. In this verse the NRSV gives "chastisement" and "punishment," with "iniquity" and "sin" as footnoted optional translations. The Hebrew terms involved call to mind *both* moral deficiency and its consequences, in this case.

*my people.* "Daughter of my people"; see the INTRODUCTION.

*without a hand laid on it.* MT *wᵉlōʾ ḥālū bāh yādāyim* is very difficult. The translation here follows the main lines of the explanation proposed by McDaniel (1968b: 45–48), who cites passages in the "War of the Sons of Light with the Sons of Darkness" (Qumran Milḥama [War Scroll], 1QM) that seem to establish a sense "attack" for this combination of words (1QM, col. 1:1; 9:1; 16:5–6; 16:7, *yḥlw ydm lhpyl bḥlly ktyym*; 17:12–14). It is perhaps best to leave open the question of the root of *ḥālū*, and the exact form to be read in this passage, whether MT or something else, since the new evidence does not seem to settle these questions. I also differ from McDaniel in preferring to understand *lō'* simply as the negative. The sense (see the COMMENT below) is that Sodom was destroyed without the extra suffering involved in a protracted siege. Other commentators have favored the same general sense, but reach it by different routes. For contrasting proposals, see Rudolph 1962; Aloysius Fitzgerald, *CBQ* 29 (1967): 368–69; and Gordis 1967–68.

7. *Her Nazirites.* Commentators have often changed "Nazirites" to "youths *(ne'ārehā)*"; the change is slight, involving only one letter, but the objections to "Nazirites" are not compelling. This could be a straightforward reference to Nazirites, that is, men under a special vow to abstain from wine and from contact with the dead, and to let their hair grow long; if not, the term may be used here in the sense of "champion, chief," as in the ancient poems Gen 49:26 and Deut 33:16, where Joseph is called the *nāzīr* of his brethren. In that case the present verse would refer to young nobles.

*Their bodies.* The usual translation for *'eṣem* in this passage, "bodies," is adopted here as fitting the context, but the Hebrew word normally means bone(s), and the translation glosses over a genuine problem. Passages in which *'eṣem* may stand for the whole person (e.g., Prov 15:30; 16:24) are not completely satisfactory parallels, since they never involve a comparison as the present text does, and since here the quality compared—redness—is rather incongruous with "bones" as the subject.

*their beards were like dark stone.* Heb *gizrātām* has long been recognized as a problem. The present translation of this rare word is not based on an etymological explanation, but on what is said in similar contexts. The word must refer to a part of the body that can be compared to a dark blue substance, probably lapis lazuli or an imitation of it. Ancient sculptors and ivory carvers often represented hair on carved heads by inlaid lapis lazuli, and ancient literature also adopts this practice in describing the appearance of gods and men. Thus Šamaš has the epithet "Bearing a beard of . . . lapis lazuli"; see Åke W. Sjöberg and E. Bergmann, *The Collection of the Sumerian Temple Hymns*, Texts from Cuneiform Sources 3 (Locust Valley, NY, 1969), line 173; on p. 87 Sjöberg gives parallels in Sumerian and Akkadian sources. Compare also Greek (Homer, etc.) *kyanochaitēs* 'dark-haired' and *kyanophrys* 'dark-browed', from *kyanos* 'dark-blue enamel, lapis lazuli'. Note also the description of Re in the Egyptian text "Deliverance of Mankind from Destruction" (*ANET*, p. 11): "His bones were of silver, his flesh of gold, and his hair of genuine lapis lazuli." If not the beard or hair, then *gizrātām* might refer to the eyebrows. In a Ugaritic epic, it is said of a beautiful woman, *dʿqh.ib.iqni.ʿp[ʿp]h/sp.trml* 'Her eyebrows are pure lapis lazuli; her eyes are bowls of jet' (Krt 147–48). The translation "eyebrows" for *ʿqh* is based on the parallelism and artists' practice referred to above; an Egyptian text also refers to eyebrows of lapis lazuli, see *UT*, Glossary no. 1906. It is conceivable that *gizrātām* is an error for *gabbōtām* 'their brows'; *gabbōt ʿēnayim* occurs once, Lev 14:9, as the word for eyebrows. Löhr proposed *nizrātām*; Weiser (1962), etymologizing *gizrātām*, translates "tattoos." Note that Paffrath translated "hair" in the present passage.

9. *Those who perished . . . field.* The Hebrew is very difficult, and the translation is conjectural at numerous points. It seems relatively certain that *mᵉduqqārīm* 'of wounds', literally, "pierced, wounded," is parallel to *ḥallē* 'slain' of 9a, on the basis of Jer 51:4; the rest is very uncertain.

10. *the food.* Heb *bārōt*, a *hapax legomenon*, is evidently a noun derived from *bārāh* 'to eat'. Since Gordis (1967–68) defends the old suggestion that MT *lᵉbārōt* conceals the designation of a Mesopotamian demon *labartu* (so also *BHK*³, notes), it may be in place to note that the Akkadian name in question has for some time been read *la-maš-tu*, not *la-bar-tu*.

12. *anyone living on the earth.* A translation "the world's rulers," based on Amos 1:5 and parallels, as understood by Frank M. Cross, Jr. and David Noel Freedman, "The Song of Miriam," *JNES* 14 (1955): 248–49, is a possibility for this passage, but Isa 18:3 and other occurrences of the phrase *yōšᵉbē tēbēl* suggest that the reference here is to the inhabitants of the earth. See Tigay 1976: 141.

13. Since the preceding verse is complete and cannot be joined to v 13, this verse, a prepositional phrase that cannot stand by itself, must be joined to v 14. Otherwise one must supply a subject and predicate, "This happened" or the like (so Rudolph 1962), but that solution seems inadmissible except as a last resort.

14. Verses 14 and 15 (together with v 13, which must begin the section; see the preceding NOTE) are among the most difficult verses in the book, and no interpretation so far proposed (including that favored here) can claim to clear up all of the problems in a completely convincing way. No review of the wide variety of proposals made by other commentators is given here, for which the reader may see Albrektson (1963) and Rudolph (1962); some previous suggestions will be dealt with in connection with individual points. Read (v 14):

> nāʿū ʿiwrīm baḥuṣōt nigʾᵃlū baddām
> bilʾī kālū wayyīgᵉʿū bā<lū> lᵉbūšēhem

(a) If one connects 13 and 14, then nāʿū is hardly said of the priests and prophets, which would be odd syntax, and must then refer to the people of Zion. (b) ʿiwrīm 'blind men' is a bit odd, but in a somewhat similar description of a catastrophe we have "they walk like blind men" (Zeph 1:17; cf. Isa 59:10; Deut 28:29). (Syriac has "her nobles," best explained as from śārīm [śrym] for MT ʿwrym [see Albrektson 1963]; this would yield good sense.) (c) Probably one should either read the niphʿal perfect nigʾᵃlū, as here, or else gōʾᵃlū, puʿal perfect, instead of the odd composite form of the MT, but cf. Isa 59:3. (d) In the second line, MT bᵉlōʾ yūkᵉlū yiggᵉʿū bilbūšēhem is really not possible, though it has been defended. Rudolph (1962): "What they were not allowed to, they touched with their garments"; others give "so that no one could touch their garments" (see Albrektson 1963 for details). (e) Redividing the consonant text, biP ī is taken to mean "by vain effort," positing the existence of a noun lᵉʾī (like ṣᵉbī, šᵉbī, etc.) from lāʾāh 'to be weary, toil'; cf. Aram lēʾū; Syr leʾūtā 'fatigue'. Both kālāh and yāgaʿ are regularly followed by b, marking the cause of the exhaustion. (f) Deleting a w, kālū is from kālāh 'to be exhausted, at an end', and is followed by a form of yāgaʿ 'to be weary'. (g) Restoring bā<lū> (lost by haplography before another l): "their clothing is tattered." If the preceding conjectures are approximately correct, the picture is of people during or just after the siege: in shock, bloodstained, exhausted, and ragged. In their filth and raggedness they resemble lepers (who were required to tear their clothes, Lev

13:45–46), hence they are depicted as giving the lepers' cry or as being greeted by the cry "Unclean!" (see the NOTE on v 15 below).

15. This difficult verse is translated as if spoken by the enemies of the Israelites, the first line being addressed directly to them, the second spoken about them. Note, however, the following problems. (a) Both lines are exceptionally long, and quite possibly the text is not in order. (b) The meaning of nāṣū is very uncertain; the context seems to require an approximate synonym of nāʿū, literally, "they have wandered." (c) Many translations join baggōyīm 'among the nations' to "they say"; the present translation takes baggōyīm with lāgūr, comparing v 20 and 1:3.

16. *The splendor of the* LORD. Literally, "the face of Yahweh." For God's face as hostile and threatening, compare Ps 34:17 [ = 16E]: "The face of the Lord is against (*b*) the wicked," and Lev 20:3, 6; 26:17; Ezek 14:8; Ps 80:17 [ = 16E]. In a famous episode God shows Moses some of his glory, but not his face: "for no man can see me and live." See Mitchell Dahood, review of Albrektson 1963 in *Biblica* 44 (1963): 548; iden, *Psalms I, 1–50*, AB 17A (Garden City, NY, 1966), first NOTE on Ps 34:17; idem, *Psalms II, 51–100*, AB 17B (Garden City, NY, 1968), third NOTE on Ps 80:17; iden "Hebrew-Ugaritic Lexicography, VIII," *Biblica* 51 (1970): 399–400. "Face (*pᵉnē*) grammatically a plural in Hebrew, is usually construed with a plural verb. Here it takes a singular verb; see GKC, para. 146a, for other cases in which a verb agrees with the rectum of the construct chain, not with the regens.

*destroyed.* On Heb ḥillēq 'to destroy' see KB³, s.v. ḥlq III, where Akk ḥalāqu, Ug ḥlq, and Eth ḥalqa are compared. See also McDaniel 1968b: 48, with references to observations by Patton and Dahood.

*He did not respect . . . spare.* Where the translation has singulars, implying that Yahweh is the subject, the MT has plurals: "They did not respect . . . spare." Plurals make of this a reference to what the conquerors did. This sense fits the general context of the book, but the shift from line 1 of this same verse, where Yahweh is the destroyer, is abrupt, and it seems better to read singular verbs here. At some stage prior to the fixing of the MT, there was a tendency to alter passages that ascribed to God responsibility for evil and calamity. It was not done systematically, and the changes that can be detected are slight. The process is well exemplified in the MT of Psalms as compared to the Psalms Scroll from Qumran (11QPSᵃ): for 119:71, MT "I was afflicted," may be compared to 11QPSᵃ "You (God) afflicted me"; for 119:83, MT "I was like a bottle in the smoke," to the 11QPSᵃ "You (God) made me"; and so on. Note that memory of another passage in the book, 5:12, may have exercised an influence here. For other examples in Lamentations see the NOTE on 1:12. Compare also the Tiqqune Sopherim.

17. *We kept awake.* Neither the *ketib, 'wdynh (*ʿōdenāh*; so also a fragmentary text of Lamentations from Qumran, 5QThrᵇ), nor the *qere, ʿōdēnū*, really yields acceptable sense, though each has been defended. Rudolph (1962) views either as acceptable. The *ketib* he understands as "they (feminine) still are" (the reference being to "our eyes"); the *qere* he explains as "we still are" ("we" going with the first-person plural suffix of "our eyes"). He would translate either "We still wore out our eyes looking," or "Our eyes still grew exhausted." But this use of *ʿōd* + suffix in a kind of absolute construction is actually unparalleled, and the explanation is ad hoc. The present translation is based on assuming a confusion of *r* and *d*; read *ʿarnū* 'we watched, stayed awake', *qal* perfect of *ʿūr*, and supply a conjunction *w* before *tiklenāh*. The assumption is that after the error of writing *d* for *r* had occurred, vowel letters then came to be written at the wrong places.

*On our lookout.* Or "From"; see Dahood, "Hebrew-Ugaritic Lexicography, VIII," *Biblica* 51 (1970): 403.

18. *They hunted . . . streets.* The translation is literal; if the MT is correct, this line might refer to a time after the city wall had been breached, when bands of Chaldean soldiers cut down anyone who set foot in the streets. Otherwise, as Rudolph (1962) suggests, following Ginsburg and Ehrlich, read *ṣārū* from *ṣrr* 'to be narrow, cramped in'; the verb occurs with the subject *ṣaʿad* 'step', also in Prov 4:12; Job 18:7; the change from *d* to *r* and vice versa is one frequently made, and translate: "Our steps were so confined we could not go out in the open." See Rudolph for a fuller discussion and other opinions. Dahood's "our feet have ranged far (cf. Ug *ṣd*) without coming into our squares" (*Biblica* 44 [1963]: 548) seems to force the Hebrew unidiomatically.

19. *were hot after us.* For this sense of *dālaq* cf. Ps 10:2.

20. *traps.* The Hebrew word is rare (only here and in Ps 107:20,

where there is a textual problem) and the form slightly suspect, but the meaning is not seriously in question, since the verb *lākad* 'to catch' is frequently used with words meaning trap, snare, net, and the like; cf. especially Ezek 19:8.

21. *O Edom.* "Daughter Edom"; see the INTRODUCTION.

22. *O Zion . . . O Edom!* "Daughter" is prefixed to each name; see the INTRODUCTION.

# COMMENT

This poem is also an alphabetic acrostic, with the acrostic figuring only in the first line of each stanza, as in chapters 1 and 2. The stanzas are, however, only two lines long, in contrast to the three-line stanzas in the preceding poems.

The content of the chapter contrasts markedly with that of earlier chapters, especially chapter 3, and one may plausibly suppose that this effect was intentional on the part of the author or editor of the book. The point of view is the same throughout, the speaker being someone who has been through the siege and fall of the city. His primary concern is to report the horrors that took place; briefer attention is given to the cause of the catastrophe, and at the very end (vv 21–22) there is an imprecation against Edom and a benediction on Zion. Although what the speaker relates is moving in its own way, the poem exhibits a relaxation of the more intense emotion of the earlier poems, and the vividness imparted there by the dramatic appearance of various speakers and especially by the personification of Zion is absent here. The tone is more matter-of-fact, closer to the actual events. In this respect it is like chapter 5, and no doubt the placing of these poems together at the end of the book was both deliberate and the product of careful reflection.

The poem consists of a series of observations, mostly having to do with the suffering of various classes of the population. There is little progression in thought, though vv 18–20 do supply a climax of action, since they seem to refer to the final flight from the city and the capture of the king. The poem is then rounded off by a threat against Edom and a word of consolation for Israel. It is scarcely possible to outline the chapter beyond a sketch.

A. A survivor's account of the siege and fall of the city, vv 1–20

    1. The fate of different groups of people, 1–17

    2. The fall of the city, the flight, the capture of the king, 18–20

B. A concluding curse on Edom and blessing on Zion, vv 21–22

The first two verses serve as a general introduction to the main theme of the chapter, the mistreatment of the people of Jerusalem. After the familiar *'ēkāh* ("How!") at the beginning, the writer creates a bit of suspense by starting off, not with a literal statement, but with a highly figurative language that is explained only in the following stanza. Gold, which as the most precious of metals is a traditional literary figure for what is of highest value, is despised! Precious stones are being thrown in the gutter. That is, he explains (v 2), the people of Zion, worth more even than gold, have been treated like worthless, broken dishes. The clay vessel, most common of ancient artifacts, as any excavation shows, was proverbial for cheapness. When one was broken the sherds were thrown out, not pieced together, and there was little regret over the loss; cf. Hos 8:8; Jer 22:28; 48:38. Compare 1:11: "How worthless I have become!"

The next eight stanzas take up the theme of famine, especially as it affected the most defenseless and dependent of the populace: the little children. As in Isa 1:3 and Jer 8:7, the people are compared unfavorably to animals. Even jackals (see the NOTE), carrion eaters who haunt deserted ruins, nurse their cubs, but the people of Israel do not feed their children and are as cruel as the ostrich. Here, of course, this indictment is ironic, for it is not the people's fault that they are unable to feed their children. If the ostrich is indeed referred to in a difficult passage in Job (39:13–18), we may conclude that it was ancient opinion that the female laid her eggs in the ground and unconcernedly left them to be trampled, so that the bird was proverbial for cruel treatment of its young.

For other ancient descriptions of famine and its effect, see 1:11, 19; also 2:11–12, and parallels cited in the COMMENT there. Failure of milk in nursing mothers (and animals) in times of siege is specifically mentioned among the curses in a Sefire treaty (eighth century B.C.): "[And should seven nurses] anoint [their breasts and] nurse a young boy, may he not have his fill; and should seven mares suckle a colt, may it not be sa[ted; and should seven] cows give suck to a calf, may it not have its fill; and should seven ewes suckle a lamb, [may it not be sa]ted," Sefîre I A 21–24, translation of J. A. Fitzmyer, *The Aramaic Inscriptions of Sefîre*, Biblica et Orientalia 19 (Rome, 1967), 15. Compare especially the curse uttered by the god Era (Era Epic IV 121): "I will make the breast dry up, so that the baby shall not live." Note also Hos 9:14 and cf. Delbert R. Hillers, *Treaty-Curses and the Old Testament Prophets*. Rome: Pontifical Biblical Institute, 1964. xix + 101 pp. 61–62.

The famine theme is continued by use of the "then and now" pattern, common in Lamentations (beginning at 1:1) and a staple element in funeral songs. Those who once could afford the best now hunt for scraps. "Scarlet clothing" was traditionally associated with being well off. D. N. Freedman calls my attention to the New Testament parallels: Luke 16:19 especially, also Mark 15:17, 20; John 19:2, 5. The entire family of the "worthy woman" of Prov 31:21 wore scarlet. It is similarly linked with "delicacies *(ma$^{c_a}$dan-nîm)*" in 2 Sam 1:24 (though there is a textual problem): Saul supplied the women of Jerusalem with scarlet clothing and "delicacies." A Mesopotamian proverb also associates a scarlet cloak with wealth (Lambert, *Babylonian Wisdom Literature* [Oxford: Clarendon, 1960], 232), and in an Akkadian ritual that speaks of a god "who has given his city away" we read "The person who had good clothing perished of cold / He who owned vast fields perished of hunger," in "Ritual to Be Followed by the Kalū-Priest when Covering the Temple Kettle-Drum," translated by A. Sachs, ANET, p. 337, text D ii 1–5. Compare *The Curse of Agade*, lines 248–53: "May that city thereby die of hunger! || May your aristocrats, who eat fine food, lie (hungry) in the grass, || May your upstanding nobleman| Eat the *thatching* on his roof, || The leather hinges on the main door of his father's house— || May he *gnaw* at those hinges!" (translation of Jerrold S. Cooper, *The Curse of Agade* [Baltimore and London, 1983], 63).

Since Jerusalem suffered so from famine during the protracted siege, the writer is compelled to conclude that her wickedness was greater than that of Sodom. Sodom also perished, but in an instant, not in long-drawn-out agony (see the third NOTE on v 6). Compare v 9: "Those killed by the sword were more fortunate than those killed by famine." Both the sinfulness of Sodom (Deut 32:32; Isa 1:10; 3:9; Jer 23:14; Ezek 16:46–56) and its sudden destruction (Deut 29:22 [ = 23E]; Isa 1:9; 13:19; Jer 49:18; 50:40; Amos 4:11; Zeph 2:9) were proverbial.

From the fate of the children, the poet turns to a group of especially sacred persons, the Nazirites (if the text and translation are correct; see the NOTES on v 7). Again the "then and now" pattern is used to show the ravages of famine. Once their skin was clear and fair; their bodies ruddy like corals, and their beards (or eyebrows or hair, see the NOTE) like dark blue stone (lapis lazuli). While details of the line are uncertain (see the NOTE), the general sense is clear. Also in Cant 5:10 the beloved is called "fair and ruddy" (ṣaḥ weʾādōm), and the lover who is speaking passes from description of his complexion (v 10) to description of his hair. In the same passage, parts of the body are compared to precious stones, as here (cf. the NOTE). On "ruddy" compare the description of the youth David (ʾadmōnī; 1 Sam 16:12; 17:42). The change in their appearance is drastic. (For the effect of starvation on the skin, cf. v 8 and Job 30:30.) Sudden death—even violent death—would have been better (v 9) than such slow wasting away from hunger (see the NOTE), which led to inhuman atrocities: women ate their own children. Although such tragedies may in fact have happened in the siege of Jerusalem in 587/586, the writer may also have been influenced by age-old literary tradition, in which the stock description of famine included cannibalism as the last dreadful state; see the COMMENT on 1:11. Since this is one of the curses for disobedience to the covenant, according to Deut 28:53–57 (which resembles the present passage in formulation), it may be that the writer intended to imply that Jerusalem was seeing the curse fulfilled because of her disobedience; cf. the COMMENT on 1:5.

As if a climax of horror had been reached, the writer turns to a more general and less vivid summary statement. Yahweh has given full vent to his anger, which in an exceptionally common metaphor is called "fire" (cf. Deut 32:22; Isa 10:17; Jer 17:27; 21:14; 49:27; 50:32; Hos 8:14; Amos 1:4, 7, 10, 12, 14; Lam 2:3, 5). The line could be a reference to the actual fire that burned down the city at the conquest, but further, "fire" is symbolic of the destructive wrath of God. This symbolism is especially apparent from the reference to burning of the city's "foundations." Since stone foundations do not burn, this is not a literal statement; it calls to mind the very similar description of Yahweh's cosmic rage, which "devours the world and what it brings forth, and burns up the foundations of the mountains" (Deut 32:22).

Since the fall of Jerusalem in 587 B.C. can scarcely have been universally noticed by all the kings and inhabitants of the earth, v 12 is not a literal statement, but a way of stating the drastic, unexpected reversal that has taken place. The theory widely held within Israel was that Jerusalem was impregnable, immune to conquest, not so much because of its actual defenses as because it was "the holy dwelling place of the Most High" (Ps 46:5 [ = 4E]). In semimythical language the psalms describe how Zion and her king by the help of God beat back the assaults of all the kings of the earth. "God is known in her towers as a sure defense. For lo! the kings assembled, and they came together. They beheld and were amazed; they were upset and put to flight. Trembling took hold of them, pangs like labor pains" (Ps 48:4–7 [ = 3–6E]). In this kind of religious thought, Zion is of worldwide, even cosmic significance, and thus at its fall, kings who stood in awe of her are thunderstruck. Similarly, in the description of the suffering and exaltation of the servant in Isaiah 52–53, the kings representing the nations are observers of the whole story.

The blame for Jerusalem's fall is assigned to her religious leaders, her prophets and priests, as also in 2:14. Here, by a bold simplification, they are said to have shed innocent blood within the city. This is elsewhere commonly pointed at as the sin of the rulers and judges (e.g., 2 Kgs 21:16; Jer 22:17; Ezek 22:6, 27) or of the whole people (e.g., Jer 7:6; Ezek 33:25; Ps 106:38–39), but here, though the writer's idea is probably not that the priests and prophets themselves laid violent hands on the righteous, he does assert that they were ultimately responsible for it by their whitewashing of injustice (cf. 2:14). The two verses that follow seem to be connected with this indictment of the religious leaders, but the Hebrew text is exceptionally uncertain (see the NOTES), so no interpretation yet proposed is free from difficulties. As interpreted by many, the unnamed subject of vv 14–15 is the priests and prophets mentioned in v 13: once "holier than thou," they are defiled by blood and are shunned like lepers. As translated here, the people as a whole are spoken of. "On account of the sins of her (Israel's) prophets . . .

(they, the Israelites are) defiled with blood," and so on. This reading seems best to fit 15b, which must refer to the nation as a whole;
but certainty is scarcely attainable in view of the textual difficulties.
In any case, the theme of defilement by blood runs through the
three stanzas, a motif well attested elsewhere. In priestly theology,
blood defiles and pollutes the land, "and no atonement can be
made on behalf of the land for the blood that has been shed in it,
except by the blood of him who shed it" (Num 35:33). Similarly, Ps
106:38–39 and especially Ezekiel (22:1–5) refer to the shedding of
innocent blood as having defiled the land and its people. In the
passage under discussion, blood shed in the past (v 13) is avenged
by the blood that now stains the people. Men wander uncertainly
in the streets like blind men (cf. Zeph 1:17), spattered with blood;
presumably the writer has in mind scenes just before the final fall of
the city, or just after the Chaldeans entered it. They are worn and
spent, and also their clothes are worn out. Their whole appearance
suggests that of lepers, and the poet pictures them as greeted by the
cry "Unclean!" People conclude that they have been shattered as a
people and made exiles for good. Like lepers they must live apart,
outside the "camp" as it were (Lev 13:46).

Yahweh has turned his "face," his overpowering splendor, toward his people in anger, not grace, and has destroyed them (v 16).
He had no respect for those one might have thought inviolable
because of their sacred office or their age, the priests and the elders.

Up to this point, a personal note has been struck only very
lightly with almost casual first-person pronouns in the stock phrase
"(daughter of) my people" (vv 3, 6, 10). Now the personal, eyewit-
ness element comes much more strongly to the fore in a series of
verses that use "we" and identify the speaker very closely with his
people. In vain, he says, speaking of the days just before the city
fell, they had worn out their eyes looking for help from Egypt (Jer
37:5–10), who once again proved herself a "broken reed" (Isa 36:6).
As we know from Jeremiah (34:21–22; 37:5–11), the Babylonian
army was at one point drawn away from Jerusalem temporarily by
the advance of an Egyptian army; as Jeremiah predicted, the relief
to the city was ephemeral. The Egyptians did not save them, and
the Babylonians returned as the prophet Jeremiah had predicted.
This and the following verses (through v 20) are often cited as
evidence against Jeremiah's authorship of Lamentations, and in-

deed it is difficult to imagine him—even for poetic purposes—assuming the pose of someone who entertained high hopes of help from Egypt, or of one who set great store by King Zedekiah.

As the siege wore on, the confinement became more and more oppressive (v 18), and it was clear that the end was near. It came when the wall was breached, ending any hope of defense. "On the ninth of the fourth month, the famine in the city had become so severe there was no food for the people of the land, and a breach had been made in the city. So all the soldiers fled, going out of the city by night by a gate between the double wall beside the royal garden, the Chaldeans being all around the city. They went toward the Arabah. But the Chaldeans pursued the king and caught up with him in the plain of Jericho, and all his army was scattered away from him, and they captured the king" (Jer 52:6–9; 2 Kgs 25:3–6; cf. Jer 39:1–5). The next verses of our poem seem to refer to this last desperate flight. It has been suggested that the author of Lamentations took part in the flight; while this remains conjectural, the vividness of the description would certainly permit such a supposition. It seems that the writer stood fairly close to King Zedekiah, and was much grieved at his capture (v 20). To be sure, he deliberately uses somewhat exaggerated language in speaking of the king, in order to sharpen the contrast between their hopes in the king and the bitter actuality. The king is called "the breath of our nostrils," an expression current in Canaan almost a thousand years earlier, as we know from the Amarna letters. This expression presumably was kept alive in the royal court in Jerusalem, though this is the only biblical use of the term. The "shadow" of the king is another of these court titles ascribing nearly divine status to the king (Pss 17:8; 91:1), just as "anointed of the LORD" (Yahweh) emphasizes the special standing of the king before God. Both terms, "breath" and "shadow," are ultimately related to Egyptian language concerning Pharaoh, the divine king; Ramses II, for example, is called "the breath of our nostrils" in an inscription at Abydos, and in another inscription he is titled "the beautiful falcon who protects his subjects with his wings and spreads his shade over them"; see Jean de Savignac, "Théologie pharaonique et messianisme d'Israel," VT 7 (1957): 82; cf. Hermann Grapow, *Die bildlichen Ausdrücke des Ägyptischen* (Leipzig, 1924), 45–46. Compare also Mesopotamian references to the shadow of the king, studied by A. Leo Oppenheim, "Assyriological Gleanings IV," *Bulletin of the American Schools of Oriental Research* 107 (Oct. 1947): 7–11. There is a poetic purpose in the use of these lofty titles, yet there is no reason to believe they are employed ironically or insincerely, especially since this passage is given prominent place as the climax of the tragic fall of the nation. It is hard to believe that Jeremiah could have written these words.

The book of Obadiah in particular provides the background for the curse on Edom that follows. "When strangers seized (Jacob's) wealth, and foreigners entered his gates, and cast lots for Jerusalem, you were like one of them" (Obad 11; cf. also Ps 137:7; Ezek 35; Joel 4:19–21 [ = 3:19–21E]). Esau, the ancestor of Edom, was the brother—in fact the twin brother—of Jacob, according to ancient tradition, and from a "brother" the conduct of Edom at the fall of Jerusalem was intolerable treachery. As in previous chapters (3:60–66; 1:21–22) the poet, though conscious of his own nation's sin, prays that divine justice will overtake the enemies of his people also. He does so here in an ironic command to Edom to enjoy herself now, for soon she will have to drink the cup of Yahweh's anger. This striking image for the divine anger is found also in Jer 13:13; 25:15–29; 48:26; 49:12; 51:7, 39; Obad 16; Pss 60:5 [ = 3E]; 75:9 [ = 8E]; Hab 2:15–16; Zech 12:2; Job 21:20. The origin and precise meaning of this imagery are uncertain, though in my opinion one may reject the suggestion made by some that there is a connection to the jealousy ritual of Num 5. There seems to be a parallel in the Sumerian *Curse of Agade*, line 230, as translated by Jerrold S. Cooper: (May certain cult figure) "Lie on the ground, like giants drunk on wine!" It may be that the image is a traditional literary metaphor, instead of having anything to do with ritual. On the subject see also John Bright, *Jeremiah*, AB 21 (New York, 1965), NOTE on Jer 35:15. The association of drunkenness and self-exposure occurs also in Gen 9:21–22; Hab 2:15–16.

The threat to Edom is interrupted by a blessing on Zion. The verb *tam* 'is complete' marks an important structural feature of the poem, the end of the alphabetical acrostic portion (see the INTRODUCTION). Apparently the verb is to be taken as referring to past time, the sense being "The worst of your punishment is over, O Zion," though in this context one might also take the perfect as precative. Although this line, even if read as a declarative sentence and not as a wish, is not yet a clear announcement of salvation for Zion (cf., e.g., Isa 40:2, "Her iniquity is pardoned"), yet it comes closer to being an expression of hope than almost anything else in the book. It recognizes that with the fall of the city and the beginning of the exile the flood tide of Yahweh's wrath had passed. Not so for Edom; her judgment day was yet to come.

# V
## A Prayer
## (5:1–22)

5:1 Remember, Lord, what happened to us;    Consider,
    and see our misery:

2 Our property has gone to strangers;    Our houses, to
    foreigners.

3 We have become orphans, fatherless;    Our mothers are
    like widows.

4 We have paid to drink our own water,    Given money for
    our own wood.

5 A yoke has been set on our neck;    We are worn out,
    and have had no rest.

6 We have shaken hands with Egypt;    And with Assyria, to
    get enough bread.

7 Our fathers sinned, and are no more.    We have suffered
    for their iniquities.

8 Slaves have been our rulers;    With none to deliver us
    from their power.

9 To get bread we have risked our lives    Before the sword
    of the wilderness.

10 Our skin has turned black as an oven    From the scorch
    of famine.

11 They have raped women in Zion;    Young girls in the
    cities of Judah.

12 Their hands have hanged our princes;    They have
    shown no respect for the elders.

13 They have taken young men to grind;    Youths have
    staggered from hard work.

14 The elders are gone from the gate;    The young men no
    longer make music.

15 The joy of our heart is gone;    Our dance has turned to
    mourning.

16 The crown has fallen from our head.    Alas that we ever
    sinned!

17 At this our heart has sickened;     These things have
    darkened our sight.
18 On Mount Zion, which lies desolate,     foxes prowl
    about.
19 Yet you, Lord, rule forever;     Your throne is eternal.
20 Why do you never think of us?     Why abandon us so
    long?
21 Bring us back to you, O Lord, and we will
    return.     Make our days as they were before.
22 But instead you have completely rejected us;     You have
    been very angry with us.

# Notes

5 Title: A *Prayer*. Not in the MT, this title is found in various Greek manuscripts; other ancient witnesses add "of Jeremiah," or "of Jeremiah the prophet."

2. After the appeal to Yahweh to remember and observe, there follows, in vv 2–18, an account of what has taken place; I have rendered Hebrew perfect verbs here mostly with English present perfects, attempting to indicate that these are events of the past, whether immediate or more remote, which continue to have effect in the present, the time when the author composed his prayer; for example, "We have become orphans" (v 3).

*property*. Namely, real property, land; the conventional English translation is "inheritance," with reference to real property held as patrimony.

*has gone*. In other words, is turned over. For this sense of *nehepkāh*, cf. Isa 60:5.

It is unnecessary to add a verb in the second colon (Haller 1940 proposed *nitt^enū* 'is given'); as it stands the line is of a perfectly ordinary type with respect to parallelism, and though the dominant meter of the poem is 3 + 3, the 3 + 2 found here occurs also in vv 3 and 14, though the latter are more evenly balanced in number of syllables per colon.

4. *water . . . wood*. (That is, firewood, as the plural form and the context implies), here in poetic parallelism, were evidently

linked together in common speech; see Josh 9:21, 23, 27; Deut 29:10 [ = 11E].

5. Read <ʿālāh ʿōl> ʿal ṣawwāʾrēnū. . . . The first two words of the line have been lost through homoioarcton (that is, through having similar beginning consonants; note that Symmachus seems to preserve a greater part of the original than does the MT); for a similar sequence cf. Num 19:2; 1 Sam 6:7. (Cf. the textual problem in Lam 1:14.) In the second colon, nirdapnū 'we are pursued' (omitted here) and yāgaʿnū 'we are weary' are a doublet; that is, the line existed in variant forms and both readings have been incorporated into the MT. For similar phenomena in Jeremiah, see J. Gerald Janzen, "Double Readings in the Text of Jeremiah," HTR 60 (1967): 433–47. Other double readings in Lamentations may occur at 1:7; 2:9a; and 3:56. "Yoke" is a common figure for servitude; cf. 1:14; 3:27; Deut 28:48; and many other passages.

6. We have shaken hands with. Literally, "we gave the hand (to)"; the sense is the same as that of the English idiom: "we made a bargain, or pact, with." The sense is probably not simply "we stretched out our hand in supplication." Compare 2 Kgs 10:15; Ezek 17:18; Ezra 10:19; 1 Chr 29:24; 2 Chr 30:8. For a depiction of kings (Shalmaneser and Marduk-zakir-shumi) shaking hands, apparently in formal confirmation of their relation as overlord and vassal, see David Oates, "The Excavations at Nimrud (Kalhu), 1962," Iraq 25 (1963): plate VIIc and pp. 21–22; and cf. J. M. Munn-Rankin, "Diplomacy in Western Asia in the Early Second Millennium B.C.," Iraq 18 (1956): 86, for possible oblique references to such an act in the Mari texts. R. G. Boling has called to my attention a possible parallel in the Amarna letter, El Amarna, no. 298, lines 25–29, where Yapahu of Gezer writes, "Let the king my lord know that my youngest brother is estranged from me, and has entered Muhhazu, and has given his two hands to the chief of the ʿApiru" (translation of W. F. Albright, ANET, p. 490). The reading "hands" is uncertain, but probable, and the parallel is illuminating.

7. The conjunction "and" is put in here for the sake of a smoother English sentence; in the Hebrew, the qere supplies a conjunction w at this place and also in front of "we."

9. sword of the wilderness. The Hebrew text, rendered thus literally, has been taken by commentators as a kind of kenning for

"bedouin," but it is difficult to insist on what the sense really is. Compare perhaps "the sons of his quiver" for "his arrows" in Lam 3:13. M. Dahood recognized in *mdbr* the root *dbr*, which occurs in the Amarna letters in the sense "drive away" and has been plausibly identified by Dahood at Ps 127:5 and 2 Chr 22:10; see his "Hebrew-Ugaritic Lexicography, II," *Biblica* 45 (1964): 401; this root would yield a translation "before the pursuer's sword." Compare also his *Psalms III, 101–50*, AB 17C (Garden City, NY, 1970), fifth NOTE on Ps 127:5, with further examples; but note the objection of Tigay 1976: 141. Others have proposed "heat" of the desert.

10. *has turned black*. This translation of *nikmārū* is based on Gr *epeliōthē* 'has become black and blue' and the meaning "be dark" of a cognate Syriac verb. Blackening of the skin from famine is mentioned in 4:8 (cf. Job 30:30). Other ancient translations, "is shriveled" and "is heated, scorched," have been defended by modern commentators; see especially Rudolph's commentary (1962), Albrektson (1963: ad loc.), and Driver (1934: 308).

11. As is normal in Hebrew poetry, the second part of this line repeats and completes what was said in the first, and one must not press the distinction between the "women" in Zion and the "young girls" or "virgins" in the cities of Judah (contrast Ehrlich 1914: VII, 53).

12. *Their hands have hanged our princes*. The Hebrew has a passive (or ergative) construction: "Princes were hanged by their hands," that is to say, by the hands of the "slaves" (v 8) who are the rulers. To avoid misunderstanding in English, this has been converted to an active form in the translation; cf. NJV "Princes have been hanged by them."

13. Both parts of the verse are difficult. The first part is often rendered as here, and it is perhaps correct, though the infinitive without *l* is a problem, and though *nāśā'* is not very commonly used in this sense (but cf., e.g., Jer 49:29). Another translation commonly adopted, "Young men had to carry the mill," is perhaps grammatically possible, and might convey about the same sense: young men had to do women's work.

The Vg translates, "Young men were sexually abused," apparently taking Heb *ṭḥn* 'grind' in an obscene sense. The verb is so used in Job 31:10, and Shaye Cohen (1982: 23) notes that the midrashic work *Lamentations Rabbati* at this point explains that the captives were subjected to sexual abuse. Scholars have pointed out a similar semantic development, from "grind" to "copulate," in other languages. In spite of the good parallel in Job, however, it is difficult to see how such a sense fits with the other half of the line.

In the second part of the verse read *bᵉʿeṣe<b>* 'from hard work', not *bāʿēṣ* 'over wood'. As Ehrlich points out (1914), the sense cannot be that youths stagger under heavy loads of wood, because *kāšal b-* means to stumble over something. "Youths stumble over wood" is hardly correct, so I have assumed a textual error: the *b* of original *ʿeṣeb* was lost from the text because of similarity to the subsequent *k*, a kind of haplography. For *kāšal b-* followed by an abstract noun, cf. Hos 14:2 [ = 1E]; Ps 31:11 [ = 10E]; Prov 24:16; in all these cases the *b* may be rendered "because of, from," as is done here.

16. For "crown" as a symbol of glory and honor, cf. Isa 28:1, 3; Job 19:9.

17. *our heart has sickened.* Cf. 1:22 and Isa 1:5; Jer 8:18. The *RSV* (so also Budde 1898, Rudolph 1962, Kraus 1968, and others) connects 17 with 18: "For this . . . for these things . . . for Mount Zion." But other examples of Heb *ʿal* plus the demonstrative pronoun *zeh* at the beginning of a sentence require interpretation as referring to what precedes rather than what follows (Jer 31:26; Ps 32:6; Isa 57:6; 64:11 [ = 12E]; Jer 5:9, 29; 9:8 [ = 9E]; Amos 8:8; while Jer 4:28; Mic 1:8; and Lam 1:16 are less clear). Furthermore, *ʿal ʾēlleh*, a plural, can only with difficulty be taken to refer to the single condition described in v 18.

18. The construction of this verse is somewhat unusual, but perhaps not totally unparalleled; the sentence type may contain what is called a *casus pendens* in traditional Hebrew grammar. One element of the sentence, in this case a prepositional phrase, *ʿal har ṣiyyōn*, is given prominence by being placed first; it is then referred to by a pronoun ("retrospective pronoun") later on in the clause (*bō*). For parallels with prepositional phrases, see 2 Sam 6:23; 1 Sam 9:20.

*foxes prowl about.* Compare a commonplace in Mesopotamian lament literature, found already in the *Curse of Agade*, 256–57): "In your fattening pens, established for purification ceremonies, May foxes that frequent ruined mounds sweep with their tails!";

translation of Jerrold S. Cooper, *The Curse of Agade* (Baltimore and London, 1983).

19. *Yet you.* The translation "Yet you" or "But you" is suggested by the use of the independent personal pronoun and the prominent position in which it is placed, whether or not one reads the conjunction *w* (not in the MT, but in most of the ancient versions).

22. *But instead.* The proper translation of this verse, important for the thought of the whole poem, is disputed because of the opening words *kī 'im* (Greek and Syriac seem to omit the *'im*, but they may have simply glossed over the difficulty; in any case *kī 'im* is preferable as the more difficult reading). The following are the possibilities: (a) Sometimes in Hebrew these two words, even in combination, retain the sense each has separately ("for if . . ."), and the conditional clause thus introduced is followed by a consequence ("then . . ."); thus Exod 8:17 [ = 21E] and elsewhere. This understanding would lead to a translation here of "For if you have utterly rejected us, you have been extremely angry with us" (so Ehrlich 1914), which is unacceptable, since the second colon does not really state the consequence of the first, but is rather a restatement of it. Note that in those cases where *kī 'im* really does mean "for if," the apodosis is usually specifically marked as such by *hinnēh* or *w*.

(b) Many translate approximately as follows: "Unless you have utterly rejected us, . . ." the implication being that this possibility is actually excluded. Rudolph (1962) defends this view by comparing Gen 32:27 [ = 26E] and states that this use of *kī 'im* is very common. Yet the passage cited, and all other cases wherein *kī 'im* has to be translated "unless" are only apparent, not genuine, parallels, for in these other cases it is used after a clause containing or implying a negative; the clause following *kī 'im* states a condition that must be fulfilled before the preceding statement can or should be in effect: "Not A, unless N" (cf. Albrektson 1963: ad loc.). The logical relation of the clauses in vv 21 and 22 is something quite different.

(c) Very similar to the preceding is the translation as a question: "Or have you utterly rejected us?" This reading is also difficult to defend, because *kī 'im* is not elsewhere used to introduce a question.

(d) The remaining possibility, adopted here (following the Vg,

Luther, the *King James Version,* and Paul Volz, *Theologische Liter-aturzeitung* 22 [1940]: cols. 82–83), is to translate as adversative: "But you have utterly rejected us. . . ." Occasionally *kī 'im* is used as an adversative conjunction even when there is no explicit negative in the preceding context; see GKC, para. 163b.

In these cases one must understand some such statement as "(the foregoing is not the case), but rather . . ."; thus 2 Sam 13:33 *(ketib)*; Num 24:22; 1 Sam 21:6 [ = 5E] (here one must translate "truly, indeed"). Here in vv 21–22, then, the sequence of thought is, "Would that you would make things as they were; (you have not yet done so), but rather. . . ." It is too much to say that such a rendering contradicts the statement of 20 and the prayer of 21 (so Rudolph 1962); it simply restates the present fact: Israel does stand under God's severe judgment. Jewish liturgical practice reflects the understanding of v 22 defended here, for it is traditional not to end public reading of this scroll with this somber verse, but to repeat after it the prayer of v 21 (see Masseket Soferim 14.2). A similar usage is followed with the end of Isaiah, Ecclesiastes, and Malachi. For other laments that similarly end in a low key, cf. Jer 14:9; Psalms 88, 89.

# COMMENT

Chapter 5 stands apart from the rest of Lamentations, especially with respect to formal features. It is not an acrostic like the other poems in the book, though it does have exactly twenty-two verses, one for each letter of the Hebrew alphabet. Metrically it is also different: it is not written in the *qinah* (lament) meter, with unbalanced lines, but for the most part in lines whose parts balance each other. The commonest line contains three accents in each half. As compared to the rest of the book, there is in chapter 5 a much higher proportion of synonymous parallelism of a segmental type, that is, of the sort in which each element in the first half-line is answered by a corresponding element in the second.

Chapter 5 is, moreover, a purer example of a recognized poetic type than any of the other poems in the book, for it follows rather closely the pattern of the "lament of the community." Probably in recognition of these differences from the other poems in the book, various Greek and Latin copies of Lamentations set chapter 5 apart, as "A Prayer," "A Prayer of Jeremiah," or the like. It is plausible to see, in this contrast between chapter 5 and the rest of the book, a deliberate editorial or authorial desire to end the work in a way that is artistically less elaborate and hence more subdued (see Grossberg 1989: 100–101).

In ancient Israel, laments of the community were evidently composed and used in times of great national distress, when the whole nation appealed for help against its enemies. Commonly cited examples of the genre in the psalter are Psalms 44; 60; 74; 79; 80; 83; and 89. Lamentation 5 exemplifies the salient characteristics of the type: the prayer is collective, making use of the first-person plural pronoun; it contains a description of the distress; and there is an appeal to God for help. Lamentation 5 is remarkable, however, for the relatively short appeal for help and the correspondingly long description of the nation's trouble; in this respect it is closer to the other chapters of Lamentations.

A.  The present troubles and their cause, vv 1–18
    1.  A call for God to notice, 1
    2.  The troubles and their cause, 2–18
B.  Praise of God and an appeal for help, vv 19–21
C.  Closing lament, v 22

The first verse, with its "Remember . . . Consider, and see," is not yet an explicit call for help, but only a preliminary: God should take notice of their distress. The word translated "misery" carries the connotation "disgrace." Ancient Israelites possessed a keen sense of honor and of the proper order of things, so that when trouble came they would complain as often and as bitterly of the shame as of the physical loss or pain, as Claus Westermann (1954: 54) points out, comparing, for example, Pss 79:4; 89:42, 51 [ = 41, 50E]; 123:3, 4.

In v 2 the translation "our property" reflects only some of the range of meaning of Heb *naḥᵃlātēnū*, which may refer either to personal estates, held as a grant from God (Josh 24:28), or to the land as a whole, "the good land which Yahweh your God gave you as a possession (*naḥᵃlāh*)," Deut 4:21, a favorite idea especially in

Deuteronomy. "Property" seems to fit the parallel word "houses" (cf. Mic 2:2). The first complaint, then, is that an order that God himself established has been overturned; both lands and houses ought to have been the inalienable gift of God (1 Kgs 21:3), and they are now held by strangers. Note the sequence "property . . . houses . . . water" (vv 2–4); Deut 6:10–11 has the same order.

"Orphans" and "widows" (v 3) were recognized in the ancient Near East as the groups of people most defenseless against agression, and this pair is linked in poetry already in very early biblical texts (e.g., Ps 68:6 [ = 5E]) and earlier still in Ugaritic poetry. Thus this line should not be made into an explicit reference to the slaughter and deportation of males; the sense is, "all of us (males included) have become defenseless."

Like "property" in v 2, so the "rest" of v 5 points to more than a physical loss. As G. von Rad in particular has pointed out, in *The Problem of the Hexateuch and Other Essays*, 94–102, an important Old Testament theological theme is that God gives his elect people rest in the promised land, especially rest from their enemies (e.g., Deut 12:10; 25:19; 2 Sam 7:1, 11). "We have had no rest" means not only "we are very weary," but "one sign of our status as God's people has been removed."

If vv 6 and 7 refer to the remoter past, then we must conclude that here a reflection on the cause of this distress interrupts the depiction of troubles. In the years just after the Babylonian conquest we know of no trafficking between Israel and Egypt. Thus *'aššur* here would be a literal reference to Assyria, a past great power, not a title for Babylon, the contemporary oppressor. This passage might then be a reference to the policy of making foreign alliances, favored by many of the kings and typically denounced by the prophets; cf. esp. Jer 2:18, 36; Hos 7:11; 12:2 [ = 1E]. These alliances were attractive to Judah not only for strategic reasons but also for economic considerations. And one could follow out this interpretive line by seeing in the phrase "to get enough bread" a link to a complex of Old Testament imagery: Israel, the wife of Yahweh, has been unfaithful with "lovers"—that is, other gods and nations—and falsely believes that these lovers are the ones who "give me my bread and my water, my wool and my flax, my oil and my drink" (Hos 2:7 [ = 5E]; cf. 1:2 above).

But perhaps the sense is, simply, "we have been reduced to

such straits that we (now) do anything to obtain food." Grossberg (1989: p. 96) suggests that "Egypt" and "Assyria" in this verse are little more than "a geographical merism." The sense would be "east and west." (Egypt and Assyria are often linked as a poetic pair even where one or the other is not especially appropriate; Egypt is mentioned first eleven out of fourteen times.)

The writer in v 7 confesses his own generation's share in the guilt of the fathers. This verse has a superficial resemblance to the cynical popular saying quoted in Jer 31:29 and Ezek 18:2: "The fathers have eaten sour grapes; and the children's teeth are set on edge," but the tone and intention is much different here: the writer does not dissociate himself from the fathers—they are "our fathers"—or from their sin. Compare v 16: "Alas that we ever sinned!" The verse expresses his understanding of, and acquiescence in, the judgment foretold in the terms of their covenant with God; the sins of the fathers are now being visited on their children (Exod 20:5). Jeremiah says much the same thing, in one verse, as Lam 5:7, 16: "We have sinned against Yahweh from our youth, we and our fathers" (Jer 3:25).

Then, at v 8, the description of the nation's distress is resumed. The "slaves" who rule are the Babylonian officials (cf. 2 Kgs 25:24), especially, one may surmise, the lower officials with whom the peole actually came in contact, and who were especially insolent and brutal. Compare Prov 30:21–22, which lists as one of four unbearable things "a slave when he comes to rule"; Isa 3:4, 12; Eccl 10:16.

Since the text refers to the lack of law and order in the land (v 9), to continued famine (v 10), and to atrocities (vv 11–12), it seems that the poem was written in the days just after the fall of the city, when conditions were still especially unsettled. The reference to Judean "princes" (v 12) is not necessarily out of harmony with 2 Kgs 25:12, which says that only the poorest of the land were left behind, for this general statement (if it is not simply poetic license) does not exclude the possibility that nobles who somehow escaped the first roundup of prisoners were later caught and executed. If it is correct to see a reference to grinding in v 13, note that grinding was a shameful occupation for a young man, work for women of the lower classes (Isa 47:2) or for prisoners (Samson, Judg 16:21).

Verse 18 is not only the end of this section, but also its climax.

Mount Zion is the central symbol of God's presence, the visible sign of Israel's election—and it is a deserted ruin. At one level, the statement that foxes have taken to prowling there expresses the idea that the holy temple is profaned by the presence of wild animals. For biblical parallels see, for instance, Isa 13:19–22; 34:11–17; Mic 3:12; Zeph 2:13–15. This is a stock element in laments over cities, and in traditional Near Eastern curses. See above, in the NOTE, and Delbert R. Hillers, *Treaty-Curses*, 44–54.

The little hymnlike verse that follows (v 19) prepares the way for the prayer that is expressed in v 20. This acknowledgment of God's eternal dominion has counterparts in other communal laments (Pss 44:2–9 [ = 1–8E]; 74:12–17; 80:2–3 [ = 1–2E]; 89:2–19 [ = 1–18]); even in the deepest trouble Israel did not forget to hymn God's praises. (The question "Why?" is a common one in national laments; see the discussion and list of occurrences in Westermann 1954.) The idea of God's unchanging sovereign might is extended in the prayer (v 21) to include an acknowledgment of his power also over the springs of human action and over human fortunes. "Bring us back" might mean "change our fortunes"; that is, it might refer primarily to an external change in Israel's situation. Or the sense may be "help us repent"; in this passage, with its "to you" (see the NOTE), this notion of an interior change is perhaps in the forefront. This, then, would be a prayer for repentance, much like "Create and make in us new and contrite hearts." One may compare Jer 31:18, which is nearly identical in its wording: "Bring me back that I may return." (Michael Barré, "The Meaning of *ľ ʾšybnw* in Amos 1:3–2:6," *JBL* 105 [1986]: 611–31 at 625 argues, following Holladay, that the *hiphʿil* of *šwb* in Lam 5:21 has the sense "bring us back into a covenant relationship"; though suggestive, this reading is perhaps overspecific.) The idea of national restoration comes to the fore in the second half of the verse.

As the poet writes, however, there is not yet any sign of favorable action by God, and the poem and book end, not in despair, yet very soberly.

# INDEX OF AUTHORS

◆

# LAMENTATIONS

# INDEX OF AUTHORS

# INDEX OF BIBLICAL PASSAGES

◆

# LAMENTATIONS